THE
MAKING OF AMERICA
SERIES

GUILFORD COUNTY
HEART OF THE PIEDMONT

By the 1930s, automobiles and streetcars shared the same thoroughfares in Greensboro and High Point. This view of Elm Street in Greensboro shows Belk, W.T. Grant, and the Jefferson Standard Life Insurance building. (Courtesy Farrell Collection, North Carolina Office of Archives and History.)

Cover: The delivery truck for F.H. Krahnke Jr. is pictured on the cover as it is parked in front of his store. F.H. Krahnke made "high grade custom clothing" and also served as a dry cleaner and alterations service. (Courtesy Farrell Collection, North Carolina Office of Archives and History.)

THE
MAKING OF AMERICA
SERIES

GUILFORD COUNTY
HEART OF THE PIEDMONT

LYNN AND BURKE SALSI

ARCADIA
PUBLISHING

Copyright © 2002 by Lynn and Burke Salsi
ISBN 978-0-7385-2367-5

Published by Arcadia Publishing
Charleston, South Carolina

Printed in the United States of America

Library of Congress Catalog Card Number: 2001093790

For all general information contact Arcadia Publishing at:
Telephone 843-853-2070
Fax 843-853-0044
E-Mail sales@arcadiapublishing.com
For customer service and orders:
Toll-Free 1-888-313-2665

Visit us on the Internet at www.arcadiapublishing.com

In honor of Dr. Donald Harris and Mrs. Jean Harris
And in memory of Jake Harris, "the Old Boy Himself"
Also for Brian, Bo, Jay, Maria, Nathan, and Margaret

The panoramic view of High Point's furniture factories in 1907 illustrates the rapid growth of the industry. (Courtesy North Carolina Office of Archives and History.)

CONTENTS

ACKNOWLEDGMENTS

A very special thank you goes to Jim Dollar, photographer par excellence, for allowing his many outstanding photographs to be used in this book. We would also like to thank the following: Steve Massengill, archivist, North Carolina Office of Archives and History; Janice Holder, archivist, Jackson Library, University of North Carolina Greensboro; Stephen Catlett, archivist, Greensboro Historical Museum; Gayle H. Fripp, assistant director, Greensboro Historical Museum; Eve Weipert, archivist, High Point Museum; Abe Jones, writer and historian; Robbie Owens, reference librarian, Greensboro Public Library; Tannenbaum Historic Park, Hoskins House, City of Greensboro; Guilford Battleground National Park; Dr. Donald Harris, for memories of his father; Mrs. Jean Harris, for history of the Harris family and the loan of photographs; Gay Shepard, librarian, and Cathy Boger, children's services, Gibsonville Public Library; Mark Drusdow, Revolutionary War historian; the Historic Jamestown Society, The Mendenhall Plantation and The Lindsay House; Charlie Sharpe, for his memories, poetry, and photographs; and Dick Douglas, for historical perspective.

We also appreciate the help of the following friends and colleagues: Connie Mason, Frances Eubanks, Barbara Springs, Andrew Martin, Jan Hensley, Nancy Bartholomew, Robin Williamson, Glenn Bolick, Chris Lynch, Mary Kaye Forbes, Nancy Quaintance, Jane Davis-Seaver, Judy Morton, Les Seaver-Davis, Carolyn R. Hines (Communications Consultant, Cone Mills Corporation), Karen Eanes and Brent L. Holmes (Proctor and Gamble), John Smith (Precision Fabrics), Lorillard, and Cathy Durbin and David Teague, the Jamestown Library.

A special thanks goes to our editor, Mark Berry, who has contributed greatly to the success of this project.

Unless otherwise noted, all photographs and illustrations are provided by the author from the Salsi family collection.

INTRODUCTION

The history of Guilford County is the history of people working together through centuries of change. No greater diversity of people existed in the settling of any other area of the state of North Carolina. In colonial times, the area was settled by various religious groups of different nationalities. All had distinctly diverse beliefs. Despite their differences, they established communities full of hardworking people, each lending his or her special talents for the good of their independent societies. At the same time, they lived in harmony side by side.

Getting a pure and total history of Guilford County is nearly impossible, for when the first settlers entered the Piedmont of North Carolina, Guilford County did not exist. At the time, the area was part of three large, backcountry counties: Anson, Rowan, and Orange. Over 20 years later, in 1771, Guilford County became a reality. Even though we begin our story at the beginning of the first settlers in the area, we concentrated our interest and research on the land area that became Guilford County.

Guilford County came into existence as a governing unit when the Royal Governor William Tryon and the Colonial Assembly passed an act for the sub-division of Orange, Rowan, and Anson Counties to create several new counties including Guilford. This appeased the area's residents, who had already fought the royal governor's troops. This act also established the parameters for choosing and designing a county seat.

The history of Guilford County is much older than the history of the Revolutionary War period that is associated with Greensboro's namesake, Nathanael Greene. Evidence of Native American settlements have been found, and it is certain that John Lawson, the royal surveyor for Queen Anne of England, traveled across the southern part of the county in 1708. So we began our story in that time of mystery and uncertainty when the first Europeans came. We have attempted to capture the history of those brave and far-sighted individuals who brought their convictions and hardworking ethics to a new land. We continued the story through the progress of railroad days, the dark days of the Civil War, and explored the coming of industry in the 1800s that continues to be an important element in the picture of the present county.

In the new millennium, history continues to be a part of the texture that is shared and interwoven with the thousands of new entrepreneurs and settlers who continue to bring their special expertise to bear on the progress and growth of the communities in the third largest county in North Carolina. Today's citizens in Guilford County do not live with the past as a daily part of their present, as do some communities in Eastern North Carolina. But thanks to the efforts of preservation societies, historical museums, churches, libraries, colleges, universities, historians, and the National Park Service, a clear picture does exist of the importance of yesterday on the progress of today.

It is with great pleasure we add storytelling to the facts, figures, and history in our quest to chronicle our common heritage. For Guilford County is part of a bond that forever connected the coastal and the mountain regions. We hope this book will make you think your own history is important.

Lynn Salsi and Burke Salsi
January 2002

Service stations sprang up in Guilford County during the 1920s and 1930s as more and more citizens turned to automobile transportation. Melvin's Sinclair Service Station was located in Greensboro. (Courtesy Farrell Collection, North Carolina Office of Archives and History.)

1. THEY CAME SEEKING LAND AND RELIGIOUS FREEDOM

The region known as the piedmont plateau is located between the coastal plain and the mountains. The word "piedmont" literally means foot of the mountain. In North Carolina, it extends east from the fall line of the rivers to the Blue Ridge Mountains in the west and is approximately 200 miles wide covering nearly half of the territory of the state. There is a vast difference in topography, in soil, and in crops that can be produced. There is also a difference in the industries that can be supported. North Carolina is made up of three distinctively different regions: the coastal plain, the piedmont, and the mountains. The coastal plain is level; as the land approaches the piedmont, it changes and gives way to gentle rolling hills.

The soil of the piedmont area represents a blending of the soils of the eastern and western regions. The difference in the climate makes the growing season longer than in the mountains and shorter than on the coast. When the first white settlers arrived, the vast virgin forests contained varieties of pine along with hardwoods of hickory, dogwood, and oak, making the clearing of land for cultivation very difficult. This abundance of wooded land actually discouraged some settlers from taking up large tracts because of the labor involved in clearing. It became a region of small farms, which were mostly cultivated by free white labor. This formed the basis of the society that lasted for over a hundred years.

The Saura and the Keyauwee Indian tribes were the first known inhabitants of the land that became Guilford County. They were among the tribes of the Eastern Sioux and were an agricultural people who engaged in hunting and fishing. It was said that they were a peace-loving people who were raided by the Iroquois. This caused the group to abandon their piedmont lands around 1711. When white Europeans arrived in the area in the 1740s, only two or three Indian families were reportedly still living there.

John Lawson, the English surveyor-general of North Carolina, arrived in Charleston from England in 1700. He traveled through the wilderness of Carolina, recorded his impressions in a journal, and ended his journey on the eastern coast of North Carolina. His travels took him through the southwestern part of Guilford County. In 1709, he published a book in England entitled, *A New Voyage to Carolina; Containing the Exact Description and Natural History of that Country: Together with the Present State thereof, and A Journal of a Thousand Miles, Travel'd Thro' Several Nations of Indians, Giving a Particular Account of their Customs, Manners.* He visited the Saponi Indians at a trading point on the

The Henry Mouzan Map of 1775 was widely used for 50 years after its creation and served as the region's most important topographic resource. Greene and Cornwallis used this map during 1781. (Courtesy North Carolina Office of Archives and History.)

Yadkin River. Then, he walked toward the east and crossed the Highwarree River to reach the Keyauwee Town on the Carraway Creek, which is near present-day Asheboro in Randolph County. He described the scene at Keyauwee as follows:

> They are fortified with wood Puncheons like Sapona, being a People much of the same Number. Nature has so fortified this Town with Mountains. That if they were a Seat of War, it might easily be made impregnable; having large Corn-Fields joining to the Cabins, and a Savannah near the Town at the Foot of these Mountains, that is capable of keeping some hundred Heads of Cattle. And all this environed round with very high Mountains, so that no hard Wind ever trouble these Inhabitants.

John Lawson stayed in the house of Keyauwee Jack, who was the king of the tribe. He was a Congaree Indian who had married the tribe's "queen." It appeared that the Indians were very hospitable according to Lawson's accounts: "At the King's house there was good entertainment of Venison, Turkies and Bears; and which is customary amongst the Indian." About their cooking, Lawson noted, "the Indians dress most things in the Woodcock Fashion, never taking the guts out." This knowledge caused Lawson and his other five fellow travelers to eat very little, however, being careful not to insult their hospitality.

The knowledge that Native Americans had inhabited the land gave the Quakers concern about the ownership of the land. They may have purchased some land from the Keyauwees, but it is thought that most of the Keyauwees had left their lands and resettled to the west long before the white man settled the piedmont. In 1764, a committee was appointed to investigate any Indian claims against lands occupied by New Garden Friends, but after two fruitless months, the matter was dropped. When Friends moved westward in 1792, a minute was adopted that "no Friend settle . . . on Indian land unpurchased."[1]

This inland piedmont territory was not one of the original factors in the history of North Carolina's development until the mid-1700s, for it was settled by an overflow of people from other states. Even after the first people arrived, it received little notice from the established communities in the eastern part of the state. Living in what many considered a vast western wilderness, these people were labeled as uncultured, rustic pioneers. This period of settlement occurred almost 50 years after the settling of the state's eastern towns of Bath Town, New Bern, and Beaufort. These settlements were located on rivers and sounds that fed directly into the Atlantic Ocean. Their citizens and businessmen enjoyed maritime trade with England, the West Indies, and other Atlantic coastal colonies. Their county governments were established and a societal core had been formed. The eastern settlers had overland routes north to Virginia and south to Charleston. They never had a need to venture westward into the wild unknown.

With no navigable waterways flowing inland from the coast, people could not travel from east to west via water. Transportation was strictly on foot, by horseback, or horse-drawn conveyance. Travel east to west was highly restricted and difficult because there were no roads connecting the areas. Also, the distance from the eastern towns to the westernmost settlements was great. Even if there had been a road, travelers would have traversed desolate forests full of potentially dangerous animals with no place to stop for refreshments or rest.

Paths and roads ran from north to south. In fact, that was one of the advantages found in settling the piedmont. There were old established, well-worn Indian paths that connected trading posts. There were also useful paths made hard packed by migrating herds of buffalo. Toward the end of the century, there was a stagecoach road between Salisbury, southwest of Guilford County, to Fayetteville, south of Raleigh, and from Salisbury to Petersburg, Virginia. With so many colonists coming from Virginia, a wide wagon road was quickly formed from the old narrow paths.

Therefore, the development of the piedmont was dependent upon settlers traveling south from Virginia, Pennsylvania, and other Northern states. The wagon road that connected Carolina with Pennsylvania became a literal thoroughfare, bringing settlers down the inland route rather than by the usual coastal waterway. This land route is popularly referred to as the "Great Wagon Road" and is recognized as the most important feature of the land rush to the piedmont of North Carolina. As people arrived, they mostly settled into farming lifestyles. Their European homelands had become hostile at times and densely populated, making land scarce. Life there had been difficult and dangerous. The Germans, Scotch-Irish, British, and Irish came to America for specific reasons, including religious freedom, the escape from political persecution, and the dream of prosperity.

The first European settlers in the North Carolina piedmont came in search of land and religious freedom. Most were part of distinct religious affiliations and had been persecuted in their homelands in Europe. The three strongest influences in the new settlements were from the English Quakers; the Germans, who were Lutherans and Reformed; and the Scotch-Irish Presbyterians. The first people came as part of a designated group with plans to work together to establish farming communities where they were free to practice their religion. The settlers were most certainly possessed by great vision and great purpose in order to transform the "middle of nowhere" to "somewhere."

Several groups arrived about the same time and brought such a diversity of talented artisans and farmers that they were able to establish successful communities very quickly. The Quakers at Cane Creek and New Garden arrived about 1745, and by 1751, Cane Creek requested to hold a monthly meeting. The New Garden families established a monthly meeting in 1752. Moravians settled Wachovia in 1753, and within a month, they had a corn mill running and two weeks later, a sawmill. The success of these communities was the best advertising Lord Granville, the last of the Lords Proprietors to own land in America, could have had for land sales. The news of the successful piedmont settlements reached the Northern colonies, and other groups arrived and settled throughout the county.

The beginning of the migration can be credited in part to a campaign by Virginia Governor Spottswood to attract settlers to the Shenandoah Valley. In 1716, the governor of North Carolina responded by offering 50 acres of free land as a homestead, and Lord Granville's company offered 640 acres for 3 shillings plus a small quitrent. At the same time, the heirs of William Penn were charging 15£ for 100 acres in Pennsylvania. The cheap prices and proof that communities could be established were incentives enough to attract vast numbers of people.

Various religious denominations first sent inspection parties to investigate the areas. They needed adequate trees to use for construction, water to power mills, available land with soil rich enough for farming, and wild game for food. These forays could take as much as two years. When satisfied with a site, the leaders returned north and organized followers to help settle the new territory. Most of the groups were deliberate and organized in their methods. They were certain to bring people with diverse skills to ensure the survival and safety of the settlement.

The Fundamental Constitution of 1669, written by John Locke and signed by the Lords Proprietors, contained a few progressive provisions including tolerance of Christian worship, the right of trial by jury, and registration of births, deaths, marriages, and land titles. The promise of religious freedom attracted thousands of settlers, and by 1700, Quakers had settled three communities in Eastern North Carolina. When Deputy Governor Robert Daniel attempted to pass a bill in 1703 requiring all assemblymen to be Anglican, Quakers refused to cooperate and blocked Daniel. The failed resolution, coupled with the migrations of thousands of settlers representing independent religious groups of many nationalities, ensured religious freedom in the county.

Women were central to the establishment of communities. Families lived in isolation and poverty. Men were involved in the almost constant occupation of conquering the wilderness. Both males and females met their responsibilities with industry and skill. In addition to bearing and raising children, cooking, cleaning, and weaving, women helped their husbands in servile work when they were needed for planting and harvesting.

Quaker women were particularly skilled. They wove for the whole family, making tow shirts, barn door breeches, and cotton dresses. They sold cloth, butter, cheese, and honey. They raised flax, cotton, and often kept silk worms. They raised sheep for their wool.

The Quaker Meeting House of the High Point Monthly Meeting became the site of the North Carolina Yearly Meeting. (Courtesy the Quaker Collection, Guilford College Library.)

Their children were brought up to be industrious, educated leaders in their respective communities. A young woman could not marry until she had 40 bed-quilts, counterpanes, and sheets. These hardworking families were self-sufficient and were able to live without much expense. They were among the first families on the frontier to set up schools, educate women, and acquire wealth.

By comparison, the men prided themselves on their physical strength. A friendly fight or wrestling encounter might be used as a test. In a company of men and boys, two men might step inside a circle on the ground and knock each other about. They boxed each other's ears as a joke, and gouged and bit each other for fun. Land clearing was backbreaking, and "log rollings" were often community events.

From the beginning, there was a large variety of wildlife to sustain the new arrivals until spring planting. There was abundance rather than variety of food until farmland could be cleared and crops harvested. There was also a degree of fear of wild animals. They were a threat to crops, livestock, and sometimes to humans. In some areas, fields were guarded until harvest. Packs of wolves were known to attack livestock and humans. Parents taught their children about the dangers of straying too far from the house. The county assemblies offered bounties for animals determined to be a danger. The North Carolina Colonial Records in Vol. XXII lists the bounties. Proclamation money was paid as follows: for every wolf, 10 shillings; for each wild cat, 2 shillings 6 pence; and for each panther, 10 shillings. The bounty was paid when the animal skin, complete with ears, was presented.

The first European people in the area settled on the Haw River in the far eastern part of Guilford County about 1745. Other groups, however, settled the area almost simultaneously. For instance, a group of Quakers settled in the Cane Creek area and then established New Garden about 35 miles away. They were followed by Friends groups at Deep River and Springfield toward the southwestern part of the county.

The Haw River people were Germans who settled near present-day Gibsonville in the far eastern part of the county, right on the Alamance County line. When Gibsonville was incorporated, one half of the town was located in Alamance County. Some were bound together by their Lutheran faith and some by their German Reformed religion. They built a small rustic church of rough-hewn logs and shared the structure. By 1745, a larger log church was built for their shared use and was known as Stahmaker's Church, and later renamed Friedens Church. Although the original log church building is no longer standing, the congregation continues to worship in the same location and is one of the oldest Lutheran congregations in the United States. The present sanctuary stands across the street from the original site. The Friedens Cemetery is the oldest graveyard in Guilford County. Until the American Revolution, the area attracted mostly German immigrants, which is evidenced by the old gravestone inscriptions in German; also, the church minutes were written in German until the 1830s. Arthur Dobbs, royal governor of North Carolina from 1754 to 1765, described the Piedmont Germans as "an industrious people. They raise horses, cows, and hogs with a few sheep, they raise Indian Corn, wheat, barley, rye, and oats, make good butter and tolerable cheese . . . they sow flax for their own use and cotton, and what hemp they have sown is tall and good."[2]

The Friedens Lutheran Church cemetery is the oldest cemetery in Guilford County. The gate stands in mute silence where it was erected in the mid-1700s. (Photo by Jim Dollar.)

A model of the original Friedens Lutheran Church was constructed of logs from the original 1745 structure. It stands across the road from the new brick church that was built in 1939. (Photo by Jim Dollar.)

The Presbyterians settled on Buffalo Creek almost in the middle of the county and also at Alamance Church toward the southeast. New members followed the first groups and each community grew around their own denominations. But the settlements remained small and far apart. They were hamlets, no more than a stop in the road, where a few families gathered to live and worship. The settlements took decades to grow into small towns. Some never grew larger than a crossroads or a stagecoach stop. Others eventually diminished until they were only a part of oral traditions.

The Quakers who moved to the piedmont in the middle 1700s, like the Scotch-Irish Presbyterians and the German Lutherans, had suffered religious persecution in Europe. They too were farmers and had immigrated for religious freedom and the opportunity to buy a great deal of land at a cheap price. The Quakers brought their English training in crafts and their knowledge of operating mills. They were also the first people to erect iron foundries in the area. Quakers owned half of the mills constructed in the county. The other half are thought to have been built by Quakers. Their skills in carpentry were also very advanced for the time. Many early families only lived in a log cabin for a short time. Mills enabled them to construct hip-roofed houses.

Many Quakers came from Pennsylvania around 1745; later in 1771, another group came from Nantucket, Rhode Island. Finally, a group of Welsh Quakers and Quakers from the eastern part of North Carolina joined the group in Guilford. The following is an account of the Nantucket Quakers from S.B. Week's *Southern Quakers*:

> The island of Nantucket being small and its soil not very productive, a large number of people could not be supported thereupon. The population of the island still increasing, many of the citizens turned their attention to other parts and removed elsewhere. A while before the Revolutionary War, a considerable

colony of Friends removed and settled at New Garden in Guilford County, N.C. William Coffin (1720–1803) was one of the number that thus removed about 1773. Obed Macy, writing of the period about 1760, says that because of the failure of the whale fishery some went to New Garden, N.C. About the outbreak of the Revolution, because of derangement of their business by the war, some went to New York and North Carolina.[3]

In 1771, J. Hector St. John DeCrevecoeur also wrote about the Nantucket immigrants in his *Letters from an American Farmer* as follows:

> They have founded a beautiful settlement known by the name of New Garden. No spot on earth can be more beautiful, it is composed of gentle hills, of easy declivities, excellent lowlands, accompanied by different brooks which traverse this settlement. I never saw soil that rewards men so easily for their labours. It is perhaps the most pleasing, the most bewitching country which the continent affords.[4]

In 1745, Nathan Dillon built a mill in an area that became known as the Friendship community on land purchased from Lord Granville. He received a license from the Rowan County Court to build a "publick" gristmill on the Ready Fork of the Haw River at the mouth of Beaver Creek. He was required by the Act of 1715 to grind all grain at a toll fixed by law. The structure was built with hand-hewn beams and a rock foundation that was laid without mortar; the mill wheel was 24 feet in diameter. In 1822, Joel Saunders moved the mill across the road from its original site, and it has been in constant use except for four

Quakers arrived in the piedmont and built many mills. The old Guilford Mill was constructed by Nathan Dillon in 1745, and it is still in operation. (Photo by Burke Salsi.)

The Quaker Meeting House at New Garden was erected in 1791. John Collins of New Jersey sketched many sights on his two trips to North Carolina. Particularly notable in this scene is the little brick schoolhouse (on the left), where the Coffin cousins taught Quaker children and held special classes to teach slaves to read and write.

years. Charles and Heidi Parnell purchased the mill in 1977, dismantled it, and rebuilt it. The mill still grinds cornmeal and operates as the old Guilford Mill on Highway 68.

New Garden Friends Meeting evolved into the most prestigious of the number of meetings that were established in the 1740s. When the first group arrived, there was nothing at all in the area—only the German settlement miles away. There was no meeting house, and there are numerous stories about leaders meeting outdoors while sitting on logs. The first meeting in a private dwelling was in the home of Thomas Beale in February 1752. By 1751, there were enough Quakers to establish a monthly meeting. It was given the name "Cane Creek," and the communities began with two preparative meetings, Cane Creek and New Garden. Though these two meetings were about 35 miles apart, the sessions of the monthly meeting alternated between the two until 1754, when New Garden was given the status of a monthly meeting.

John and Mary Payne were among a small group of families who immigrated to New Garden from Virginia in 1766. Their daughter, Dolley, was born on March 20, 1768. She grew up, married James Madison, and became the first lady of the United States when he was elected to the presidency in 1809. John and Mary Payne only lived in the area until 1769. However, Guilfordians are proud to claim their county as the birthplace of one of America's most famous women.

Another Quaker group established a community on the Deep River. They chose the area for economic reasons because they were interested in harnessing the waters of the

The simple interior of the Quaker Meeting House was sketched by John Collins. Men worshiped on the right, and women, on the left. (Courtesy the Quaker Collection, Guilford College Library.)

Deep River to saw wood, grind grain, and turn lather. They are attributed with creating Guilford County's first manufacturing area. Deep River owes its parenthood to the New Garden Friends Meeting. In 1754, the older meeting granted permission to Friends at Deep River for a meeting to be held regularly at the home of Benjamin Beeson, except when it was held at Mordecai Mendenhall's residence. They erected a log meeting place in 1758 using the Quaker pattern with a movable partition separating the men's and women's business sections.

The settlement became the center of an active community engaging in trade and local industry. Most of the development was about 4 miles away from the meeting house; however, the people came by horse, wagon, and buggy to worship at Deep River. This settlement grew and the citizens later named it Jamestown in honor of James Mendenhall, a miller who emigrated from Pennsylvania in 1750.

By 1771, Richard Beard arrived in the area and brought with him the tools to establish a hat shop and tannery. The hat shop gained fame, and frequently, the Beard's Hat Shop was used as a point of reference when describing where locals lived. Richard's son, William, learned the trade from his father and passed it on to his son, David Beard. The hat shop became a trading post for hunters, who brought furs to the Beards in exchange for supplies. One end of the shop was also used as a general store.

By the late eighteenth century, several brick buildings faced the federal road that ran through Jamestown, making it the first place in the county to have the appearance of a town. Jamestown was designated as a polling place in the late 1790s and granted a state charter in 1812. People traveled long distances to purchase products from the sawmills, gristmills, potteries, tanneries, stores, and hat shop.

The tavern, also called an ordinary, was an important institution. Before 1741, tavern keepers obtained a license from the governor, and after that, from the county court. Applicants had to exhibit good character and competence "to keep good and sufficient Houses, Lodging, and entertainment for Travelers, their Servants, and Horses." In the 1750s, distilling was a chief industry. Whiskey, brandy, and cider were made throughout the state and was often used as payment for goods. There was generally a liberal flow, for no gathering was without spirits, including funerals. Moderate drinking was universal; however, drunkenness was considered inappropriate and was disdained by polite society.

Bruce's Crossroads was one of the early settlements in the northern part of Guilford County. In 1769, Charles Bruce, a Scotsman, who had first settled at Buffalo Creek, purchased a great deal of land for a reasonable price and moved about 10 miles north to build a homestead. Gradually, others gravitated to the area, and the crossroads became a stop for people traveling north to Danville and west to Salem. On their journeys, they passed Bruce's house and the area became Bruce's Township.

Many settlers arriving from Ireland first landed in Pennsylvania. They found that most of the large tracts had been taken and that the available land was much more expensive than they had anticipated. They headed south, purchased affordable land, and supported their families by farming and by working at their crafts. A large group of Scotch-Irish

This colonial structure, the home of Philip Hoggatt, was built in 1754 and is the oldest structure in High Point. Hoggatt was an early Quaker potter. (Photo by Burke Salsi.)

were sponsored by a Presbyterian Church in Lancaster County, Pennsylvania, to travel to North Carolina. They claimed 20,000 acres of land. The deeds to the land on North Buffalo Creek and Reedy Fork Creek date to 1753. In 1756, the group constructed a church near Buffalo Creek and named it Buffalo Presbyterian Church.

The Alamance Church was settled near Birch Creek. John and Marianna Paisley were Irish immigrants who came from Pennsylvania. They became members of David Caldwell's congregation and their son, William Denny Paisley, was born in 1770. When he was older, he studied with David Caldwell and was licensed as a home missionary in 1795. He later returned to Guilford County and was the beloved founder of the First Presbyterian Church.

By 1765, neither the Buffalo Presbyterian Church nor the Alamance Presbyterian Church had a minister. They joined together and invited David Caldwell to become their minister. Caldwell was a native of Pennsylvania; he was appointed to come to North Carolina as a missionary. He had only recently become an ordained minister at the age of 40. After working as a master carpenter for years before "answering the call," he was assigned to "labor at least one whole year as a missionary in North Carolina."

Before moving to Orange County, he married Rachel Craighead of Mecklenburg County, 17 years his junior, and brought her to help him farm 550 acres. In addition to farming and carpentry, he also operated a gristmill to supplement the $200 per year he earned as a minister. Mark Drusdow, Greensboro historian, pointed out that the $200 was a combined salary of both churches. Caldwell was often paid in tradable goods rather than cash because there was a lack of hard currency in circulation.

Caldwell ultimately influenced the history of the area more than any other single person. He lived to be 99 years old and served as a minister at Buffalo Presbyterian and

The Buffalo Presbyterian Church used two sanctuaries between 1756 and 1827 before the structure seen here was constructed of handmade brick. In 1919, the David Caldwell building was added to the left, and the Rachel Caldwell building was added on the right in 1952. (Photo by Jim Dollar.)

The Buffalo Presbyterian Church cemetery is adjacent to the church and is the oldest cemetery in Greensboro. It is the final resting place of David and Rachel Caldwell and veterans of the Revolutionary War. (Photo by Jim Dollar.)

Alamance Presbyterian from 1768 until 1820. Both of the churches were organized before his arrival; however, he was the first pastor to serve both churches.

David Caldwell and his wife adapted well to the backwoods environment. Historian Mark Drusdow believes their Scotch-Irish heritage prepared them for hardships in the wilderness. Caldwell rose to the occasion to minister to his flock, assisted his fellow man, no matter what, and provided for his own family. Upon his arrival, he realized that there was no school and no doctor. His first home was a frame two-story structure. The family's living quarters were located on the first floor, and in 1767, only two years after his arrival, he organized a classical school and located it on the second floor of his house. According to Drusdow, "Caldwell became the best known and most sought after teacher south of the Potomac."

Caldwell built a log structure to house the first academy in the area to educate young men. It was referred to as the "Log School," since most schools of the day were one-room log structures. He enrolled approximately 50 students a year and many of the graduates went on to influence the growth of Guilford County and of the state. Governor John Motley Morehead was one of his best-known graduates.

David Caldwell eventually became a self-educated physician because there were no doctors in the area. He secured medical texts and learned the profession through reading. He increased his knowledge through corresponding with an old college friend, Dr. Benjamin Rush, of Philadelphia, the leading physician and medical authority in America at the time. Caldwell's services as a doctor continued even after he was in his nineties.

Andrew Gibson immigrated to America with his father from Edinburgh, Scotland. At the age of 15, he first went to Charleston and then to Cheraw, South Carolina. He moved to Guilford County about 1775 and opened a general store. He married Jane Freeland of Orange County, and they had eight children. He acquired a great deal of property, as well as a number of slaves, and was thought to be "well to do." The family did extensive farming and gold mining, which was considered the earliest industry in the Friedens Church area. Shafts were dug 50 and 60 feet deep and the area was known as "Gold Hill."

Unlike the Quakers, who were pacifist and peaceful, the Scotch-Irish were sometimes agitators, evolving into soldiers and outspoken politicians. These men eventually fought and died during the Revolutionary War. The Germans had come from the Palatine area of Germany and escaped from their homeland, where the Thirty Years' War had left terrible devastation. For years, their lack of speaking English kept them from elective office.

The Baptist came to the county in 1755, settling in Sandy Creek in what is now Randolph County. Reverend Shubal Stearns, an ordained minister of the Separate Baptist, had "felt the call" to carry the gospel to other parts of the country. He left New England with a small group of followers and settled for a short time in Virginia. Friends encouraged him to travel to North Carolina, telling him that "preaching is desired by the people." Stearns and his followers traveled 200 miles south and established the Sandy Creek Baptist Church. Eight families worked together to establish a community and preached the gospel of "being born again." The membership grew to 606 people. The church sent forth evangelists and within a few years, 42 churches and 125 ministers sprang forth in Virginia, North Carolina, and South Carolina. Reverend Stearns conceived of the idea of organizing an association. In 1758, all of his churches sent ministers and delegates to the annual association meeting.

The Baptists were very active in Rowan/Orange County prior the War of the Regulation. They fought with the Germans and Scotch-Irish to preserve their rights. But many left for Tennessee—to escape the political dissension—never to return to the "Regular Country."

With the three different and distinct nationalities in the same area, they were still far enough apart that by means of horseback or walking, it would have been a long distance

The Isley House represents the earliest type of construction in the county. In 1973, the house was moved to the Greensboro Historical Museum, and it serves as a memorial to Dolley Madison, who was born in a log house. (Photo by Burke Salsi.)

to travel. Needless to say, the Quakers, Germans, and Scotch-Irish did not socialize nor did they intermarry. Each was governed by his own commitment to his faith and his place within his own family and thus, within his community. Because the area was devoid of evidence of any former culture and history, the new people were able to easily establish the culture and customs of their heritage and homelands. Although the three groups lived side by side in harmony, there was an eventual clash of ideas. The disagreement festered only after prosperity was established—the question of slavery was looked upon with divergent points of view. The Scotch-Irish had come to the New World and were willing to defend their freedom even if it meant bearing arms.

The dissension that eventually arose in the piedmont was mostly due to the unorganized, confusing, and downright illegal way in which Lord Granville conducted his business. When seven of the Lords Proprietors surrendered their charters to the King of England in 1728, John Lord Carteret, later the Earl of Granville, retained his one-eighth interest in the land. No steps were taken to lay out his share until 1742, when the King directed the appointment of commissioners to make the necessary survey.

In order that Granville might have his estate in a solid tract, the commissioners decided to locate it wholly in North Carolina. The North Carolina–Virginia boundary was the northern line of the Granville district. The Granville District ended up becoming an immense region, covering 26,000 square miles, and in 1744, contained two-thirds of the inhabitants and wealth of North Carolina.

Granville maintained an office in Edenton with agents, surveyors, entry takers, and other officials. Corruption was rampant and scandalous. Also, it was usual for grants to overlap. With Granville in England, agents were involved in the collection of illegal quitrents and fees. For decades, money and land were disorganized. Quitrent money went directly to Granville's pocket or to his agents' personal incomes. Therefore, much revenue never made it into the public treasury. This dual territorial and fiscal system was another source of political division.

Governor William Tryon represented the King of England and therefore, kept his eye on the settlements throughout the state. In a letter written in August 1766 to the Board of Trade, located in the Colonial Records of North Carolina, Vol. VII, Tryon made the following comments on the settlements in the west:

> I am of opinion that this province is settling faster than any on the continent. Last autumn and winter upwards of one thousand wagons passed through Salisbury with families from the northward, to settle in this province chiefly; some few went to Georgia and Florida, but liked it so indifferently that some of them have since returned.
>
> The dispatch of patents I have granted since my administration will show to your Lordships the great increase of settlers in the western or back counties. These inhabitants are a people differing in health and complexion from the natives in the maritime parts of the province, as much as a sturdy Briton differs from a puny Spaniard.

Tryon regarded the western territory "as of great value, being perhaps the best lands on this continent." This was after 20 years of settlement. By this time, communities were

The blacksmith shop was integral to each piedmont community. This blacksmith shop, built in the mid-1700s, is located at the High Point Historical Museum. (Photo by Burke Salsi.)

coordinated. The people, who dared to move into a desolate area with nothing but their intelligence and brawn to carve out a lifestyle, had to be hardworking and unafraid of difficult and backbreaking labor. By then, many families also had comfortable homes. They worked their crafts and their lands successfully from sunup to past sundown. In the temperate climate, they grew fields of wheat, corn, buckwheat, and patches of flax and cotton.

In 1773, Governor Martin complained that the Granville District created a division in the colony, which for many years had "fatally embarrassed its Policies." The governor, the assembly, and the people felt the entire state needed to come under one government—the Crown. In 1773, the assembly petitioned the King to purchase Granville's District. Nothing came of the suggestion, for the Revolution came, and the British left the colonies. The problem of the Granville District was solved by confiscation of land by the Patriot government.

From almost the beginning of the settling of the county, many residents, particularly the Quakers, were concerned about the moral, political, and commercial effects of owning slaves. In the early colonial years, there were no slaves in the county. As the number of immigrants increased, some brought slaves, and as the size of farms grew, slaves were introduced into the Guilford communities.

The distribution of slaves in North Carolina followed agricultural patterns. On the eve of the American Revolution, 40 to 60 percent of the households in North Carolina owned slaves. However, most of the slaveowners were located in the eastern counties, the area with larger farms. In counties in the western part of the state, slaveholdings were relatively insignificant. Only 10 percent of the households owned slaves.

In contrast to the eastern counties, the western counties supported a large free Negro population—approximately 11.6 percent of the Negro population was free. There was also a small number of Negro indentured servants. Free blacks served in the militia with no apparent discrimination until the nineteenth century, when they were limited to the role of musicians. Until their disfranchisement, free black men voted in North Carolina from the Revolution until 1835. However, so as not to sound positive about the status of the free blacks in western counties, they faced tensions between races because of competition for available jobs. Free black men faced more taxes and often were confronted with the threat of becoming enslaved.

And, despite the better conditions for blacks, there were farmers who owned slaves. Figures indicate that about one-third of the farmers owned 10 slaves or less, with only a few farms operating with more than 25. The very well-respected Reverend David Caldwell and John Motley Morehead were slaveowners. However, the entire Quaker community was steadfastly against slavery. Quakers who owned slaves did so as a technical ownership. They took custody of slaves until they could arrange to free them. They operated a school for slaves and taught them trades so that they would be able to support themselves when a way to freedom was found. Most Quakers who owned slaves freed them in 1774.

The Friends objected to the practice of slavery well before the Revolutionary War. A protest against slavery occurred in 1688, and it was recorded in the Philadelphia yearly meeting. In 1715, the New England Yearly Meeting made slaveholding a disownable offense. It was natural when the Quakers settled the new territory that they rejected any members who had sold or owned slaves. When freeing slaves was declared against the law in 1830, it presented a big problem for the Friends.

In 1771, there were 22 counties in the eastern part of North Carolina; there were only 7 in the west. Yet, half of the population lived in the seven western counties. Most members of the legislature (General Assembly) were approved by the royal governor and lived in the east close to New Bern, where the new Governor's Palace was built. Therefore, the imbalance in representation caused great conflicts.

Traveling to the county seat to carry out personal business such as paying taxes, recording deeds, attending court, and performing land transactions was time consuming and expensive due to the great distance. Those who lived in the area that became Guilford had to travel on foot or by horseback to the county seat in Hillsborough, at least 35 miles in one direction. Those who lived in Rowan had to go even farther to reach Salisbury, the county seat.

Suspicions developed because of the difference in lifestyles in the east and the west, the difference in nationalities, and the difference in religious beliefs. The tensions all climaxed when a tax increase was levied to pay for the construction of a palace in New Bern for Royal Governor William Tryon. All of this set the stage for the event called "The War of the Regulation."

Besides being a spiritual leader and doctor in the county, David Caldwell became an arbitrator between Royal Governor William Tryon and the Regulators at Alamance Creek. As an Ulster-Scot, he was very familiar with what he felt was English harassment. His family had come to America for freedom and was among a group who were determined to stand up to tyranny. He was known for supporting and encouraging self-determination.

Therefore, when he came to North Carolina, he supported his congregations' conflicts with unjust taxes and the royal government's dishonest enforcement. He first took up the fight by writing Governor Tryon a letter, which was ignored.

The "war" was more a struggle for representation by the settlers living in the frontier areas than it was a "war." The residents of Rowan and Orange felt that they were victims of discrimination and looked at the royal taxes as a burden they had to bear to support politicians in the east. They deeply resented receiving no benefits. The group named themselves "Regulators" and refused to pay taxes that they felt were illegal.

After the General Assembly authorized military action, Governor Tryon called out the North Carolina militia. Members of David Caldwell's churches, Buffalo and Alamance, joined the Regulators, as did the German Lutherans and the Baptist. The Regulators met the governor's volunteer militia on a field of conflict at Alamance Creek near the Alamance Church on May 16, 1771.

Tryon promised Caldwell that he would not fire upon the Regulators, of whom many were only equipped with farm tools or simply unarmed. However, he did open fire on them. Nine men on each side were killed and fifteen prisoners were taken by the royal troops during the two-hour battle. The governor offered clemency to those who would agree to come under the royal authority and take an oath of loyalty to the King. Even though the royal governor's militia was the winner of the two-hour battle that ensued, the event shocked North Carolinians, giving them greater determination to be free from the rule of King George.

On January 26, 1771, the colonial assembly had met at New Bern and passed "An Act for erecting a new County between the Towns of Salisbury and Hillsborough" by taking part of the Orange and Rowan Counties. Four new counties were formed: Guilford, Wake, Chatham, and Surry. With the creation of the new counties, all of the residents gained additional legislative representation. This had not stopped the hostilities that erupted in Alamance, mainly because the bill had not yet passed and the assembly had authorized the governor to use military force. The act passed immediately after the War of the Regulation and accomplished the ultimate end of the struggles. The new county was named "Guilford" for Francis North, the first Earl of Guilford, whose only son, Frederick, presided over the cabinet of Great Britain between 1770 until 1782. The earl was a member of Parliament and a personal friend of George III and Queen Charlotte.

The first Court of Pleas and Quarter Sessions met on May 14, 1771, at Robert Lindsay's house in the Deep River community. Seven commissioners were appointed to conduct the business of the county. The court was set to meet in February, May, August, and November.

The days of the county courts most often coincided with muster days and sometimes a county fair. The court was held to decide lawsuits and settle differences. "Muster Day" increased the activity, and many came to meet friends, exchange news, talk politics, settle accounts, trade horses, and buy and sell provisions. People came from miles around to race and jump horses. Often there were also wrestlers and marksmen who would match their skills with others.

The early people of Anson, Orange, and Rowan Counties were mostly hardworking farmers. They cleared the land, rotated crops, and were diligent in planting and harvesting.

Governor William Tryon is shown confronting the Regulators prior to the Battle of Alamance. (Courtesy North Carolina Office of Archives and History.)

It was unfortunate that the state was not well connected by roads. This made selling produce very arduous. Since it was so expensive to transport produce, most families grew little more than the family could eat.

Few goods were transported; however, there was a great deal of going and coming up and down the wagon road from north to south. Those with relatives in northern settlements were known to plan trips north more easily than they could to other cities in their own state. Once established in the Piedmont Plateau, they found travel to the valleys of the Yadkin in the north and the sand hills of South Carolina easier than to the eastern towns of their own colony.

Thus, it developed that the markets of the piedmont section of North Carolina were not New Bern, Fayetteville, and Wilmington, but Camden, Columbia, and Charleston in South Carolina. In 1768, a resident of Mecklenburg County protested against the erection of a governor's palace at New Bern. He gave among the reasons for his attitude that "not one man in twenty of the four most populous counties will ever see this famous house when built, as their connections and trade do, and ever will, more naturally center in South Carolina." Many local farmers and merchants believed the popular axiom of the day, "The products of the soil determine the occupations of men, and the means by which they earn a living influence their political opinions."[5]

By 1775, the population of North Carolina was scattered from the Atlantic Ocean to the Blue Ridge and beyond. There was tremendous growth due to natural increase and through the immigration of thousands of people settling in the state.

2. Rights of Government and the People

Between May 1771 and 1774, citizens of Guilford County enjoyed a peaceful period of some economic independence and renewed purpose. The threat of a full-blown war with the Regulators was seemingly over, and seven commissioners set about establishing the new county.

Justices of the peace took oaths of office at Robert Lindsay's house in May 1771. They decided a 2 shilling poll tax should be levied for three years to finance a courthouse, prison, and stocks. They appointed commissioners whose duties included selecting a location for the courthouse and dividing the county into districts so that citizens could begin working on the roads. They also made plans to keep up the bridges and clear rivers and creeks.

The boundary lines defining the area of the county were established by June 19, 1771, but it took almost three years before a site for the courthouse was agreed upon. County commissioner Alexander Martin, of New Jersey, had moved to Guilford County, was admitted to the Bar in 1772, and was also in favor of moving the site of the county seat from Robert Lindsay's place on the Deep River.

In 1774, the county commissioners purchased a 1-acre parcel of land from John Campbell, another county commissioner, and erected a courthouse. It was to Campbell's advantage to have the courthouse on his property. The new site became the county seat and became known as Guilford Courthouse. The following year, Alexander Martin and Thomas Henderson bought 100 acres next to the courthouse.

The citizens finally had representation in the assembly and had a new county seat; however, they were disgruntled that in the same act for the new county, they were still destined to go to Salisbury to attend proceedings of the Superior Court. They were also required to pay a poll tax of 6 pence toward the construction of a new courthouse building. At the same time, a "fence-in" law was enacted and each planter was required to fence in the cleared land that he had under cultivation. The citizens simultaneously experienced fair representation, yet felt the full impact of county rules and regulations.

Tensions increased over acts that continued to be passed by the British Parliament since 1763. To make matters worse, Royal Governor William Tryon was sent to New York and Josiah Martin arrived on August 12, 1771, as his replacement. Martin was a terrible selection and his overbearing demeanor, petty tyrannies, and tactless personality further pushed the state into rebellion.

Alexander Martin served as one of the first commissioners. He was also a representative to the Constitutional Convention and a governor for North Carolina.

A meeting was called for counties to send representatives to New Bern on August 20, 1774, to attend the First Provincial Congress. It was the first assembly in America for the sole purpose of defying King George III and the Royal Governor Josiah Martin. Guilford was one of five counties that did not send delegates. Some historians believe that representative were not sent because one-third of the population of the county were peaceable Quakers. Also the Presbyterians, Baptists, and Lutherans still suffered from emotional and personal conflicts left over from the War of the Regulation. Since the former Regulators had taken oaths of loyalty to the King, they were hoping to retain the status quo.

In an address to Governor Josiah Martin in 1775, John Fields, a former Regulator, expressed the loyalty the people of Guilford felt to his Majesty and it was signed by 116 of "His Majesty's most loyal subjects of the County of Guilford." Many who took the oath "never to bear arms against the king" let it be known that they would honor their oath even though they sympathized with the "friends of liberty." It was about this time that Reverend David Caldwell counseled former Regulators and personally absolved them from their oaths. It did not take long for David Caldwell to become very unpopular among Tories, those people still loyal to the Crown.

A Committee of Safety was appointed to govern North Carolina. It was designed to provide executive authority to enforce the policies of the Provincial Congress. The first Congress recommended "a committee of five persons be chosen in each county." The committee was established in each town, in each one of the counties, one in each of six military districts, and one for the province at large. The committees met with just enough opposition to allow them a display of firmness. Nothing could give citizens whose loyalty was questioned immunity from an inquisition—not wealth, not position, and not poverty.

Social and commercial ostracism was the favorite weapon, and few had the courage to withstand it. Up until that point, the people of the state barely supported "the cause." The strength for "a fight" with the crown came mostly from the eastern settlers who were English and Highland Scots. The Scotch-Irish and the Germans did not care to be part of their quarrel.

In March 1775, the people in the eastern part of the state became aware that Governor Josiah Martin had contacted the British government about taking force against the people. He was so closely watched by the Committee of Safety in New Bern that he feared being seized. In May 1775, he fled the palace at night and on June 2 sought protection at Fort Johnston, located along the Cape Fear River. Martin renewed his activities to the extent that Whigs in the Cape Fear area became alarmed and resolved to drive him out of the fort. He learned of the planned attack and escaped three days before the Minute Men burned the fort to the ground.

In May 1775, when news of the Battle of Lexington reached North Carolina, the Committees of Safety shed every drop of allegiance for the Crown, organized drills, and equipped troops. War between those loyal to the British king and Patriots was on the mind of all citizens.

The second Provincial Congress met on July 2, 1775, in Hillsborough to make preparations for war. It was fully attended. The delegates agreed to raise two regiments as part of the Continental Army and six regiments for each of the six military districts. Funding was a problem, so paper money—$125,000 bills of credit—was issued. They decided to change from the English pound to the Spanish milled dollar. Eight shillings to the dollar was set as the standard of value. Anyone not accepting the bills in payment or changing the established rate was to be considered "an enemy of his country." Counterfeiters were to "suffer death."

As the situation grew worse, a great deal of bias was shown toward known Tories. Political strife became intense and bitter. Thinking the majority of citizens would remain steadfastly loyal, Royal Governor Martin remained offshore in a British ship. He sent commissioners to Guilford County and throughout the piedmont to rally troops to march to Brunswick in the eastern part of the state. Before the Tories departed from Guilford, a skirmish occurred between them and Patriots. Captain William Dent, of the Patriot cause, was shot and robbed. Similar incidences caused "fence sitters" to become Patriots.

During the colonial development of the state, all white males between the ages of 16 and 60 were enrolled in the militia. They were required to attend four company musters and one regimental muster a year. There were three muster grounds located in Guilford County. With Whigs versus Tories, it was imperative to the Patriot movement to convince able-bodied men to shed themselves of years of military service to the royal government and sign up to fight against many men who were their friends and sometimes other family members.

During the fourth Provincial Congress in Halifax in July 1776, the members received news of the adoption of the Declaration of Independence. Representatives were urged to return home and proclaim the Declaration in a public manner. The fifth Provincial Congress met in Halifax beginning in November for six weeks to adopt a constitution. The five delegates from Guilford County included Charles Bruce, Ralph Gorrell, and

David Caldwell. On December 17, a Declaration of Rights in 25 articles was adopted. On December 18, 1776, a Constitution for the State was adopted. Richard Caswell was appointed as the state's first governor.

Many citizens did remain loyal to the King and signed up when the Royal Governor Josiah Martin began raising troops to control North Carolina; the going was not easy. Resistance was raised at Bruce's Crossroads, where Charles Bruce was active in recruiting Patriots to resist the King's troops. In 1769, he had moved away from the more populated area of Buffalo Creek and built his home away from other settlements. As an inevitable war drew near, he ardently mustered out militia for the Patriot cause. His home was the headquarters for military men and politicians. Just prior to the Battle of Guilford Courthouse, the Bruce house was headquarters for "Light Horse" Harry Lee and was the site of a skirmish between the troops of Lee and British Colonel Banastre Tarleton. Tarleton's men killed Lee's young bugler, James Gilles. The British soldiers responsible for his death were captured, executed, and buried somewhere near the Bruce place. Following this encounter, the Royal troops organized and marched to Moore's Creek Bridge in Eastern North Carolina. There, the Loyalists soundly defeated the Patriot forces.

In 1776, the Provincial Congress authorized Charles Bruce and Daniel Gillespie, both residents of Guilford County, to collect arms for Guilford troops, which would be under the leadership of Colonel James Martin. According to Gladys Scarlette in her book *Summerfield, North Carolina: A Pictorial History*, Bruce continued recruiting men for the Continental Army during the war and received 1 shilling for each recruit. Land was so cheap in that area of Guilford County that 12 shillings would purchase 640 acres. After the war, Bruce served as a commissioner and surveyor of confiscated property. He added to his fortune by accepting a fee of 2 shillings per acre.

The Daughters of the American Revolution erected this monument in Summerfield (Bruce's Crossroads) to honor Charles Bruce and James Gilles, who are both interred at the site. (Photo by Burke Salsi.)

Between 1776 and 1778, the Southern colonies were seemingly free from the enemy. However, nothing was further from the truth. In the summer of 1776, North Carolina helped to raise 14,000 troops for the defense of Charleston. During the same summer, there was a bigger worry. The Creeks and the Cherokee Indians took up arms and laid waste to the borders of Virginia, North Carolina, South Carolina, and Georgia. The four states raised 6,000 armed men who went against the Indians and forced them to agree to peace. In addition to the war, the county suffered from the differences in philosophy of the Quakers, who would not bear arms. They were repeatedly double-taxed and harassed in many physical and personal ways. The political philosophies of the Whigs, the Tories, and the Committee of Safety were constantly at odds. In 1779, land was confiscated from residents who were loyal to the King. In the same year, Guilford County was divided again; the southern part of the county became Randolph County. After a second division in 1785, the county was approximately one-third the size it had been in 1771.

In the summer of 1780, Georgia and Charleston, South Carolina, surrendered to the British. It became apparent that the British would enter North Carolina. The leader of the British forces in the Southern campaign, Lord Charles Cornwallis, was convinced that the best way to ensure the security of South Carolina was to invade North Carolina. North Carolina had become a sanctuary and staging ground from which the Patriots launched destructive raids and refitted troops. The remnants of Horatio Gate's Patriot army had retreated to the town of Hillsborough, east of Guilford, to recuperate and attempt to recruit more men. In Cornwallis's mind, the subjugation of North Carolina would eliminate two threats. Cornwallis felt that failure to achieve this would inevitably force the British to "give up both South Carolina and Georgia and retire within the walls of Charleston."[1] Lord Charles Cornwallis had already soundly defeated Horatio Gates at Camden, South Carolina. He felt he could easily do it again in the state of North Carolina and ultimately reclaim North Carolina for the British.

General Nathanael Greene, a Rhode Island Quaker and a close colleague of George Washington, was persuaded to take over command of the Southern army in Charlotte in December 1780. He described the men of his new command as "a few, ragged half-starved troops in the wilderness, destitute of everything necessary for either comfort or convenience of soldiers." From this group, Greene fashioned a force that would successfully elude and engage the King's troops.

Patriot General Daniel Morgan went to South Carolina while General Greene remained in North Carolina. Greene's strategy included moving closer to provisions and reinforcements in Virginia before engaging the British. Greene's move to Virginia caused the British to move farther from their supply lines and forced them to live off the land.

General Greene passed through Guilford County on his way to Virginia. When faced with a showdown with the British, he determined that the area around Guilford Courthouse would be a suitable place to engage the British. On March 14, 1781, the village of about 300 people gave way to armies of 4,000 men. Greene's familiarity with the topography gave him the opportunity to prepare a battle plan. He set his men into three fixed lines. General Cornwallis moved his army north to attack. Fighting was vicious and terrible. When the British were closing in on the Patriots, Greene decided to save his army by retreating. He withdrew to the northern part of the county. He sent his baggage up the

General Nathanael Greene led the Patriot forces against the British at the Battle of Guilford Courthouse. Greensboro (originally called Greensborough) is named in honor of the general. (Courtesy North Carolina Office of Archives and History.)

road toward Bruce's Crossroads, causing it to be locally referred to as the "Old Baggage Road" for 200 years. Even though he gave Cornwallis the victory, Greene regathered his troops and marched to South Carolina, where he was instrumental in ousting the British the next year.

Although the battle was a tactical victory for the British, they sustained a greater loss of officers and men. The Quakers treated the wounded of both sides at the New Garden Meeting House and in many private homes. The McNairy house near the thick of the fighting was the site of an operating room where Dr. David Caldwell struggled to save lives from both sides. In the aftermath, New Garden Friends faced the task of burying the dead and caring for an overwhelming number of wounded. Some of these wounded soldiers were carriers of smallpox. Shortly afterward, General Cornwallis left for Randolph County. Regarding the heavy losses of the British troops, British statesman Charles James Fox commented, "Another such victory would destroy the British Army."

There is a story of a New Garden Quaker who was so enraged when British foragers plundered his farm, that he volunteered for Greene's army for the day, explaining to his wife that he was going hunting. It was discovered that this "Friend" did not rejoin his Quaker community until sometime after the Battle of Guilford Courthouse.

The Quakers were severely handicapped by the foragers of both armies. When General Greene appealed to the New Garden Friends to care for the wounded, they complained that they were "ill able to assist as much as we would be glad to as the Americans have lain much upon us, and of late the British have plundered and entirely broken up many of us." However, true to their Quaker beliefs, they "made no distinction as to party or cause" and cared for both Americans and British wounded and dead.[2]

The American Revolution ended with the signing of the Treaty of Paris on September 3, 1783. Land that belonged to Lord Granville's heirs and to those sympathetic

33

Revolutionary War reenactments are a regular part of programs at the Guilford Courthouse National Military Park. Mitchell L. Hunt (center) is shown with his Continental line unit, Kirkwood's Company Delaware, at a reenactment of the Battle of Guilford Courthouse. (Courtesy Mitchell Hunt private collection.)

to the King was confiscated and sold. At that time, Alexander Martin, Charles Bruce, and Thomas Henderson were among the politically connected who purchased hundreds of acres of confiscated property, including 350 acres near the Guilford Courthouse.

In May 1787, when the constitutional convention was held, 55 men representing all of the states except Rhode Island met in Philadelphia to design the new government. The North Carolina General Assembly sent delegates William R. Davie, Richard Dobbs Spaight, Governor Richard Caswell, Alexander Martin, and Hugh Williamson. William Blount replaced Governor Caswell. Four out of five of the representatives were from Eastern North Carolina. Alexander Martin, of Guilford County, represented the state's western interests. On September 17, 1787, 39 of the 42 members present signed the Constitution for ratification by individual states.

In July 1788, the state Constitution convention met in Hillsborough to consider North Carolina's adoption of the U.S. Constitution. Guilford's five representatives included David Caldwell and Daniel Gillespie. Since it did not include a Bill of Rights, the delegates voted against ratification of the Constitution. The population of most of the state of North Carolina and all of Guilford County was still comprised mostly of farmers. There was a general fear that small farmers would be overlooked by the new government's vision and control. The members who were anti-Federalist feared the power of "big government" versus the people. This left North Carolina outside of the United States until a Bill of Rights was adopted. Another convention was held in Fayetteville in November 1789, and North Carolina then became the 12th state in the Union.

The practices and procedures of county government remained the same and were basically unchanged from colonial times. The court of common pleas and quarter sessions was still the locus of power. The General Assembly and not the governor and his council, as in colonial days, appointed justices. Some county offices, such as sheriff, were elective, but a small group of men held most of the power. It was not a truly representative government even though men had fought and died for it.

The founding of the courthouse helped to establish attorneys and encouraged people to move to the new community. In 1787, Andrew Jackson moved to Greensboro to live with the Francis McNairy family to read law with their son, John. They had become friends while studying in Salisbury, after which Jackson "read" at the home of Charles Bruce. The McNairy home was close to the Guilford Courthouse, where John McNairy and Jackson became licensed to practice law. When Tennessee opened for settlers, the friends sought appointments in the new territory. John McNairy became a superior court judge and Andrew Jackson became a prosecuting attorney in the same district.

In 1782, Alexander Martin was elected governor of North Carolina and a new village was laid off around Guilford Courthouse. It was named Martinville in his honor and also because he was one of the largest landowners. It remained fairly small from 1785 to 1808, and never grew any larger than a village, with only one street named for General Greene. The local county commissioners in 1785 were William Dent, a surveyor; Ralph Gorrell; Robert Lindsay Jr., who ran the general store and was a coppersmith; John Hamilton;

The Francis McNairy House, constructed in 1762, was originally located only a mile from the Guilford Courthouse. Andrew Jackson read law with McNairy's son, John, and resided in the house prior to receiving his license to practice law on November 20, 1787. The structure was restored and is now located on the site of the old Lindsay Street School adjacent to the Greensboro Historical Museum in Mary Lynn Richardson Park. (Photo by Jim Dollar.)

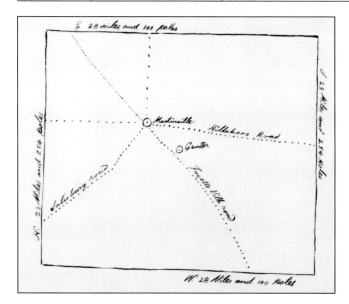

The hand-drawn surveyors' map shows the locations of Martinville and the soon-to-be new town called Greensborough, marked center. (Courtesy North Carolina Office of Archives and History.)

and William Dick, who owned a wagon factory and blacksmith shop along with Bazilla Gardner and Alexander Martin.

The Revolutionary War laid a foundation for the future of the state, but population growth slowed considerably. The war slowed immigration from Pennsylvania and Nantucket, which for years had been the chief sources of recruits for North Carolina Quakers. The growth of German Reformed, Baptists, Lutherans, and Moravians also slowed. This was generally a brief period of very slow growth in other areas of the state as well.

However, all denominations profited when the Anglican Church's influence was diminished. Following the Revolutionary War, the bishop of the Church of England failed to appoint a bishop for the new nation. Many former Anglicans were discouraged with their religious affiliation. Protestant faiths found great growth with the new atmosphere of total religious tolerance.

Land prices rose, and there was a period of land speculation. Paper towns sprang up in every section of the state. In fact, between 1783 and 1789, the legislature incorporated 29 new towns, many of which were never settled. Dozens of acts for the purpose of stabilizing business conditions were passed during these years. However, few of the acts addressed the need for proper thoroughfares connecting the eastern and western sections of the state. For decades to come, the citizens remained divided politically and economically.

3. DEVELOPMENT OF TRADING CENTERS

The modest number of cities or even small towns as trading centers contributed to the backwardness of the state. People with goods to sell or merchants who wanted to stock their shops were obliged to go outside the state. Lack of trade clearly was a serious obstacle to the development of North Carolina.

Despite the lack of good roads, President George Washington caused quite a stir in 1791, when he came to Guilford County as part of his Southern tour. He wanted to view the battlefield at Guilford Courthouse, where his cousin William Washington and his friends, Nathanael Greene and Harry Lee, had distinguished themselves during the Revolutionary War. Washington spent the morning at the battlefield and then had dinner with Charles Bruce at his home in Bruce Township. The first President spent the night with former governor Alexander Martin.

In 1790, the first United States Census stated that Guilford County's population was 7,291—including 3,406 white males, 3,242 white females, 27 free persons, and 616 slaves. Most people lived and worked on farms. North Carolina ranked third in population, with Virginia and Pennsylvania being larger. However, within 20 years, the state narrowly held fourth place, and there were only seven towns with more than a thousand people in the entire state.

Even though the county had experienced little growth, in 1801, there was a move to locate the county seat in a more suitable central location. It was generally felt that if the courthouse were placed closer to the geographic center of the county, then it would be of greater convenience to the population. When Randolph County and Rockingham County were cut off from Guilford, the county seat and thus the courthouse needed to be relocated. A great controversy ensued.

Based on the testimony of surviving witnesses of 1805–1807, General M. Logan, clerk of the county court, supplied the following information for the *Greensborough Patriot*:

> There was great strife, and contention and canvassing throughout the county of Guilford on a proposition to remove the seat of justice from the ancient and battle-scarred town of Martinville, and to establish a new metropolis at the centre of the territory. The population became arranged under jealous leaders into two opposing divisions . . . the Martinsville Party and the Centre Party. It would fill a volume, or at least one of the largest sort of chapters in history, to

Horse-drawn covered wagons brought thousands of settlers to the piedmont and were a principal form of transportation for over 200 years. (Courtesy University Archives and Manuscripts, Jackson Library, the University of North Carolina at Greensboro.)

describe and bring up in review before the reader the drivers hard arguments and sharp-pointed remarks which were hurled like javelins, arrows, and sling stones between the opposing hosts. It was a time that tried men's soles—in traveling about into all manner of nooks and corners of the realm, gathering recruits for the wordy war.

At length the Martinsville Party determined on . . . a right slick proceeding that was expected to throw the Centre Party . . . But alas! For the short-sighted wisdom of mortal man; this scheme wrought out their own speedy defeat. Having procured an enactment of the county court and forever establish the metropolitan supremacy of Martinsville. But this enactment and decree only served to redouble the vitality of the Centre Party, bringing out their latent talent and force. And on an accurate toll of the noses they were found to comprise half the population and a little more. So the new decree went forth and the glory departed from Martinsville and it was left from that time to decay among the bones of the dead who had fallen in the old battle of Greene and Cornwallis.

In 1807, commissioners decided to have a brick jail and new courthouse built in Martinville. There was great opposition to the building of a courthouse that was not in the middle of the county. An election was held in August to determine the location of the county seat. A group named the Centre group won. On December 16, 1807, seven commissioners were named to find a suitable location. They were William Armfield, David Caldwell Jr., Charles Bruce, Hugh Forbis, Jacob Clapp, George Swaine, and Nathan Mendenhall. Petitions are still preserved in the archives at Raleigh dated in October and November 1807. They are signed by hundreds of citizens after "We the undersigned."

Mendenhall was the surveyor. He found the actual center of the county to be a marshy area that is now a section of land located in a park in the Fisher Park neighborhood. Because the land surveyed to be at the center of the county was low, marshy, and considered unfavorable for construction, the location of the new county seat, without a name, was located close by on the crest of a nearby hill. The land was owned by Ralph Gorrell, a prominent landowner and former legislator.

The county's growth had everything to do with the relocation of the county seat to the newly created town in the county's geographic center. The area was totally unpopulated and devoid of any structures, yet the move created excitement and land speculation.

On March 25, 1808, Gorrell agreed to sell 40 acres for the construction of the courthouse at the price of $98. The new town commissioners announced the sale of

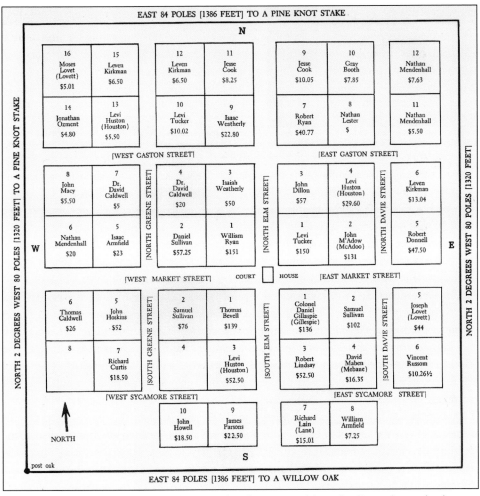

Nathan Mendenhall, a surveyor, laid out the plan pictured here for Greensborough, the new county seat. The original courthouse stood in the intersection of Market and Elm Streets. (Courtesy North Carolina Office of Archives and History.)

The Genesis Monument was erected in east Fisher Park to mark the exact center of Guilford County and the original proposed site for the new county seat of Greensboro. (Photo by Burke Salsi.)

lots so that money could be made available for the construction of the jail, stocks, and a whipping post. Nathan Mendenhall drew up plans for a village that would be square, one-fourth mile wide and one-fourth mile long. Four streets were laid out and referred to as North, South, East, and West. Then the lots were sold at auction.

Thirty-three men purchased 44 lots at prices from $4 to $151. The courthouse was to be located in the middle of the four streets with the entire village radiating two blocks in each direction from the courthouse square. The auction raised $1,689.39.

On December 15, 1808, the general assembly passed an act naming the county seat "Greensborough." David Caldwell Jr., a commissioner, suggested the name to honor General Nathanael Greene. At the time, it was spelled "Greensborough"; however, it is not known why the third "e" was left off the name of the town. It was not until 1895 that Greensborough spelled with the "borough" was shortened to "Greensboro." The editor of the *Patriot* probably played a part in dropping the "ugh" because he often published the name as "Greensboro'."

A courthouse building was completed in 1809, and on May 15, it was used for the May session of the Court of Pleas. The new structure symbolized such permanence and stability that new residents were attracted to the area looking for opportunity and some rural residents moved into town. A few wealthy citizens established their main residence in town while keeping their old house on the farm.

With the development of Greensboro as a county seat came the organization of a local government. The first town charter was adopted in 1810. The state legislature passed an act that contained 13 sections relating to the governing of the new town. It named six men as commissioners of police to preserve law and order. The town was thereafter referred to as "incorporated." In 1824, Greensboro became a self-governing town, for the state legislature no longer appointed the commissioners.

At the time, there also was much banter concerning dueling. On Wednesday, May 24, 1826, the *Greensborough Patriot* stated as follow:

> There is scarcely any subject on which more discordant opinions are entertained than on that of duelling; and whilst one party condemn it as a flagrant violation of all the laws both of God and man, others are contented to represent it as a necessary evil.

Conduct of citizens was on the mind of city and county officials and was also of concern to the more elite residents. In the Wednesday, August 26, 1826 issue of the *Greensborough Patriot*, the following notice was posted concerning jurors:

> The Grand Jury of this County, last week, presented a Juror for being intoxicated in the jury box, and the Court fined him fifty dollars; the fine is to be remitted to one dollar, if the Juror will prove to next Court that he has kept sober since the last term.

In 1829, the commissioners selected William Adams as constable and John M. Logan to be the town's first "Publick" officer, tax collector, and census taker. It was a part-time job that paid $15 a year. All men, ages 21 to 45, were required to participate as citizen patrols to assist the "Publick" officer. Each company of men volunteered to serve for a week. In 1839, the city hired a night watchman to help patrol from 10:00 p.m. until sun up at a salary of $1.15 per week.

In April 1829, Greensboro's first code with nine regulatory ordinances was adopted:

> 1. Every person who shall exhibit a Stud horse in any part of the Streets of this town nearer to the Courthouse than the first Cross Street Shall be Subject to a fine of Five Dollars . . .
> 2. Any person Known to Keep Wood, Stone or Lumber in the Two Main Streets Crossing at the Courthouse . . . unless for the purpose of Building . . . for Twenty-Four hours shall be fined Two Dollars . . .
> 3. Every Person living within the Incorporation Shall be Subject to a fine of Five Dollars For Every Ten Days his Chimney or Chimneys Shall Remain Less than Two Feet and a half above the Comb of his house . . .
> 4. Any Person Known to drive or stop a Wagon Cart or Carriage of any description in any Street within the Corporation at any publick time For the purpose of Selling any Article or Commodity What Ever, Shall be fined One Dollar . . .
> 5. Any Waggoner or Other Person who May feed his team of horses Within the Two Main Street Crossings at the Courthouse Shall be fined one dollar for such offence . . .

6. Any Person known to fire a gun or Pistol (the Cannon Excepted) any where Within the Corporation shall be fined one dollar . . .

7. Any Person throwing Shavings, Straw, Leather, Ashes, or any other kind of litter in the Streets shall be fined one dollar for every Such Offence . . .

8. Any person Watering a horse at Either of the Publick pumps shall be fined one dollar . . .

9. The officer of Police Shall at times attend to the Removals of any Nuisance when Required by any of the Commissioners under a penalty of One Dollar for each Neglect. [1]

In 1830, the commissioners adopted a tenth ordinance establishing a fine of $1 for feeding a hog in any of the town streets. They also established a night patrol. There was a curfew for blacks, slave and free, that did not apply to whites. In 1833, the commissioners of police began a system of fire protection requiring each household to clear its yard of rubbish and to have two ladders, one of which would reach the roof's peak.

The earliest public buildings in Greensboro belonged to Guilford County. The first courthouse that was completed in 1809 was used for almost ten years. Guilford militia met there to enlist volunteers. When the *Patriot* began publishing, announcements for the militia appeared stating, "Parade at the Court House square on Friday at 10 o'clock, completely armed and equipped for inspection." In May 1818, a new courthouse was constructed; however, it became dilapidated and was replaced by 1828. Other new facilities included a jail, whipping post, stocks, pillory, and place for executions. In 1845, a new jail and an office for the county clerk were built.

In 1837, the general assembly passed a new charter. Greensboro was reincorporated, a tax schedule was adopted with $5 as the maximum real estate tax, and the official city limits were extended so that the town covered 1 square mile. New wells were dug as a town service to keep disease at bay. Citizens were regularly drafted for street work.

In 1839, the town commissioners replaced the night patrols of regular citizens with two hired watchmen. A beautification program was begun when elm trees were planted on the streets leading from the Courthouse Square. Mr. Gill, an African-American man, was paid $34 to plant the trees in the spring of 1840. The commissioners set a fine of $50 to be paid by anyone caught playing cards within the town boundaries.

In 1845, a typhoid fever epidemic caused a public health furor. A marsh east of town was drained, and Greensboro gained a short-term reputation of being an unhealthy place. Many out-of-town academy students did not return to classes, and the Caldwell Institute was forced to move to Hillsborough.

Greensboro began to look like a progressive town in 1849. William Caldwell and Lyndon Swaim, editor of the *Patriot*, organized a volunteer fire department. A hand-pumped fire engine was purchased in Baltimore for $600 and a brick firehouse, 18 feet by 28 feet, was constructed near the courthouse. Despite much progress, mostly in the southwest part of the county, there was little progress in constructing additional roads to connect the various villages within the county. Greensboro and Jamestown were the only settlements that looked like towns. Greensboro was boosted by its status as the county seat and Jamestown was considered an industrial trade center.

Born in Greensboro, Dolley Payne Todd Madison, wife of the fourth President of the United States, is remembered for her efforts in saving valuable papers and works of art from the White House during the War of 1812. (Courtesy Greensboro Historical Museum.)

Earlier in the nineteenth century, as Greensboro was growing as the county's industrial and social center, the average Guilford citizen attempted in every way to "tune out" any attachment to the War of 1812; it was far away and did not affect them. Unfortunately, it was impossible to ignore. The Embargo Acts of 1807 forced Americans to make items at home they had formerly purchased abroad. This caused people to become more independent. When the war was over in 1814, no one wanted to return to the old ways, and this gave rise to a new era in political, social, and economic attitudes.

When Norfolk, Virginia, was threatened with a British invasion, a call was issued for men in Guilford County to respond. The Guilford Militia did not want to hold a draft. Members were called to the courthouse and asked to volunteer. No one stepped forward, and Dr. David Caldwell was requested to preach. Writing on August 4, 1852, of his memory of the momentous occasion, John Motley Morehead remembered "to have seen the old gentleman, then eighty-eight years old, literally crawl upon the bench of the court house to address the multitude and in fervid and patriotic strains exhort them to be faithful to their country." Reverend Eli Caruthers, who had come to Greensboro to assume David Caldwell's ministry, reported that "His very appearance on such an occasion and for such a purpose, was enough to inspire the young and vigorous with patriotic ardor and heroic intrepidity." Caldwell's plea was so effective that two companies were raised.

During the war, in 1814, Guilford citizens were proud to learn of the efforts of former citizen Dolley Madison, wife of President James Madison, who saved valuable papers and a portrait of George Washington from the White House while the British were burning and looting Washington, D.C. The county also received reports about Andrew Jackson's illustrious victory at the Battle of New Orleans in 1815.

By 1820, Guilford County had seven main roads traversing the area and converging in Greensboro, yet travel conditions could only be described at best as rugged. There were no amenities; travel was accomplished only by those who really needed to visit the courthouse.

Stagecoach service connected Summerfield, Greensboro, Jamestown, and High Point to Virginia and points south and west. (Courtesy North Carolina Office of Archives and History.)

Even in the decade from 1830 to 1840, no other region of equal area along the Atlantic Seaboard could have exhibited to the patriotic citizen so discouraging a prospect or so hopeless an outlook. Citizens traveling through the area would have found public roads and means of transportation as primitive as they were when the American colonies acknowledged allegiance to King George III. Delays, inconveniences, and discomforts were the least of the evils that beset the traveler who entrusted life and limbs to public conveyances; such a traveler might reach his/her destination if he/she did not break his/her neck in the effort. The cost of transportation was so great that the profits of one-half the planter's crop were consumed in getting the other half to market. A legislative committee reported in 1842 that the freight rate by wagon between Raleigh and Petersburg averaged $1.50 per hundred pounds. The freight on a 500-pound bale of cotton between those two points would be $9. The freight on a sack of salt was $2. Many farmers found it profitless to produce more than their own families could use. As late as 1853, a traveler within 30 miles of Raleigh saw "three thousand barrels of an article worth a dollar and a half a barrel in New York, thrown away, a mere heap of useless offal, because it would cost more to transport it than it was worth."[2]

Travel in Guilford County was eased slightly when a scheduled stagecoach service was established in the county in 1839 to accommodate travelers. Most of the passengers were "drummers," or salesmen, calling on storeowners and doctors. Many people came to Greensboro for court business and to engage one of the many attorneys who had established a practice. Travelers created a demand for accommodations, and inns were established to provide refreshments and lodging at major crossroads or near the small communities along regularly traveled routes.

In fact, stagecoaches provided the only dependable transportation for travelers who did not have their own vehicles. Stagecoach travelers were mostly people of means who preferred the comfort of an overnight stay in an inn. Those who were poor had to travel the best way they could and camped out beside the road at night. Over the years, areas evolved into campgrounds of a sort where regular travelers knew the location. From the earliest colonial times, many ordinaries, or taverns, accommodated a few travelers; however, after the Revolution, more inns were established offering more refinement than a tavern. In 1786, Jonathon Welch purchased a substantial brick Quaker house on Patrick's Creek and converted it into an inn. The Towmey's Inn was located at the intersection of the Cape Fear Road. The Brummel's Inn was situated south just over the Davidson County line.

In addition to providing a much needed service, stagecoach owners offered various sightseeing excursions for those who could afford entertainment and luxuries. These tours increased their revenue on established mail routes. During 1840, the *Patriot* carried the following advertisement on June 16, 1840, for the Tri-Weekly Line, which was owned by Kent and Bland:

> Travel from Greensborough and Lexington, N.C. to the Virginia Springs.
> Persons wishing to visit the famous Virginia Springs are informed that they will
> find prompt stage accommodations either at Greensborough or Lexington, N.C.
> Our stages reach each of the above places every Sunday, Wednesday, and Friday
> connect in Salem and proceed thence to the Gray Springs, Gray Sulphur, Red
> Sulphur, Salt Sulphur, and White Sulphur Springs three times a week and back.
> Visitors from the east will find no difficulty in securing seats at Greensborough
> and those from the South at Lexington. Both these points are on the daily mail
> route between Raleigh and Salisbury. Passengers are informed that they will find
> every accommodation and attention calculated to make them comfortable on the
> road and will be broken of their rest but one night on their passage.

Greensboro historian and author Ethel Stephens Arnett noted that in 1849, the stagecoach fare from Goldsboro to Charlotte was $18 and the travel time was 84 hours. Peter Adams was Greensboro's stagecoach magnate, and his lines had six-horse coaches that ran in several directions.

Between 1815 and 1850, approximately one-third of the population migrated to Tennessee, Alabama, and Ohio. In 1829, a newspaper correspondent in Asheville reported that from 8 to 15 wagons passed through that town everyday bound for the west. One day, in 1845, the editor of the *Greensboro Patriot* counted 19 wagons from Wake County passing through Greensboro on the way to the west. The 1850 Census revealed that 31 percent of all the natives of North Carolina then still living in the United States were actually living in other states. People left for many reasons, including the indifference of the people and politicians to education, neglect of natural resources, such as the wearing out of farmland, reluctance to levy taxes for public services, general backwardness, and opposition to slavery. Some wanted more land at a cheaper price and others sought opportunity. The state's political, economic, and social climate drove away approximately 405,161 people. About 58,000 people specifically moved to states where slavery was prohibited.

Much of the exodus from Guilford is attributable to the Quakers' intolerance of slavery. They made many efforts to expand the chances of freedom for slaves. In Guilford County, they formed the North Carolina Manumission Society as an organization of Quakers, reluctant slaveowners, and others who were interested in abolition. They affirmed their belief in the truths in the Declaration of Independence, especially citing "all men are created equal." The group was organized on July 19, 1816, by Charles Osborne, a Quaker minister from Tennessee, a birthright member of Centre Meeting. The first delegates represented New Garden and Centre Friends Meetings. The society was active for 18 years, and over that period, 1,455 delegates were appointed to its sessions. Their main objective was helping slaves gain freedom and assisting them to learn how to support themselves once they gained freedom. They also felt they could eventually affect enough influence on the state's political system that the laws could be relaxed enough to desist from the harassment of freed slaves and that little by little, all slaves would be freed.

By 1826, the Society of Friends sponsored an annual meeting of the Manumission and Colonization Society. Members voted for manumitting all "colored people" held by them that were willing to leave the country. They presented several plans to carry their intentions forward. These Southern abolitionists announced that among the manumitted people that they encouraged to find freedom, 120 wished to go to Haiti, 316 to Liberia in Africa, and about 100 wished to be sent to either the non-slave holding states of Ohio or Indiana.

Richard Mendenhall chartered the vessel that sailed in July 1826. Dr. George Swain traveled to Beaufort to attend to the embarkation of those who wished to travel to Haiti. Those who chose to go to Liberia were to leave by the first vessels that were sailing to the African settlement. Those wishing to move to Ohio or Indiana were taken in wagons. All were freed and sent to their destinations at the expense of the Society of Friends.

Mrs. Mary Mendenhall Hobbs shared her memories with author Sallie Stockard in 1902. She recalled that the chartered ship was named the *Sally Ann* and was captained by Captain Swain of Guilford County. She also related that the Manumission Society purchased many of the slaves that they freed.

George Mendenhall and his family were instrumental in the founding of Jamestown and the development of the entire county. (Courtesy the Quaker Collection, Guilford College Library.)

*Richard Mendenhall educated slaves and
allowed them to run his store, which was
located across the road from his house. (Photo
by Burke Salsi.)*

About that time, George C. Mendenhall, a prominent Jamestown Quaker, was the
largest slaveowner in the county. He owned as many as 100, but didn't think the custom
was civilized. According to Sallie Stockard, the "Negroes on Mendenhall's farm" were
trained as special craftsmen in carpentry, harness making, shoemaking, tailoring, cooking,
and agriculture, and they reached a high state of perfection in their crafts.

Stockard wrote the following about his slaves:

> His slaves were all special workmen. Being taught a trade, they worked at it, not
> running around from one thing to another. In his store, a Negro clerk sold and
> bought goods. His harness shop was kept by a slave who was a harness maker
> and whose harness took first premium at the State Fair before the war. His
> carpenter helped to build the capitol at Raleigh. His caterer was sent to wait on
> President Buchanan when he visited the University of North Carolina. George
> Mendenhall had a shoe shop; a work shop in which were made plows, rakes,
> hoes and a large flouring mill, cotton gin, tanyard, and farm, all worked by
> specially skilled slaves.[3]

Mendenhall set up a school just for slaves so that they could learn to read and write and
become independent citizens. As soon as they could be fitted for emancipation, they were
transported by him to free soil.

Quakers purchased slaves as a manner of having custody until they could arrange
their freedom. This was considered technical ownership. Many Quakers who found
themselves in the position of helping slaves became members of the Manumission Society
or cooperated with them. The Guilford County Quakers were not alone in their mission
to free slaves. They were supported financially by Friends groups throughout the United

States and in Europe. They got a great deal of editorial support from publishers of the *Patriot* newspaper. William Swaim, who purchased the paper in 1829, was particularly vocal about his abhorrence of slavery and let it be known that he was an active supporter of the Manumission Society.

It must have been distressing to those in opposition to slavery when they read frequent notices in the local newspaper concerning slaves for sale. The publishers were not at liberty to refuse this type of advertisement for fear of being punished by law. From the beginning of the paper in 1826 until the Civil War, advertisements ran similar to the following piece that was published in the Saturday, December 22, 1827 issue of the *Patriot and Greensborough Palladium*:

> Negroes for Sale
> Will be sold to the highest bidder, on the first day
> of January next, in the town of Greensborough,
> on a credit of twelve months, the slaves belonging
> to the estate of Z. Swain, deceased. The slaves consist
> of a valuable man and two women. All persons
> indebted to said estate are notified that unless they
> make immediate payment, their notes and accounts
> will be placed in the hands of an officer; and those
> having claims are requested to present them.
> Signed by A. Geren, Ex'r.

At a semi-annual meeting in March 1829, the General Association of the Society took an inventory of itself and concluded that it had not accomplished all it had wished, but that it had done enough to justify its continuance. They decided to combat the deep-rooted prejudices, the ignorance, and the sordid avarice of people by publishing a special address to all branches of society and to the citizens of North Carolina through William Swaim's newspaper.

The address took a year to write. When published in a small book, it was entitled *An Address to the People of North Carolina, on the Evils of Slavery*; its authorship was attributed to "The Friends of Liberty and Equality." It was also widely known that William Swaim was the author. On March 10, 1830, Swaim began printing excerpts in the *Patriot*. It was highly regarded by the opponents of slavery and it was reprinted for 30 years.

In 1830 and 1831, highly restrictive legislative measures were passed blocking every method a person could use to carry out freeing a slave, including a number of acts directed against the individual slave. Free Negroes were prohibited from preaching to colored congregations. It became illegal to educate a slave and it was against the law to free a slave. Most free black people, in fear of being enslaved, left the state. Furthermore, the Quaker Law of 1830–1831 required male members of the Friends to either report for military duty or pay a fine. There was such a mass exodus of Quaker families from the state of North Carolina that the Manumission Society held its last meeting in 1834.

Also in 1834, Quakers at the yearly meeting issued a protest to the general assembly stating their opposition to the oppressive laws prohibiting the education of slaves. Up

The Mendenhall House, built by Richard Mendenhall, has been a landmark in Jamestown since 1815. It was a working farm, a stagecoach stop, a tannery, and an integral stop on the Underground Railroad. (Photo by Burke Salsi.)

until that time, Quakers held to the belief that slaves should possess basic literacy and should learn a trade so when freedom came, they would be able to support themselves and enjoy a dignified life. The school begun by Levi and Vestal Coffin in 1821 in the little brick schoolhouse adjacent to the New Garden Meeting House had to be discontinued.

The state government's pro-slavery stance literally drove Quaker families from the state between 1800 and 1860. The blow to the Quaker population of Guilford County was devastating. Entire communities packed up, lined up their wagons, and left. Many resettled in Ohio and Indiana, where slavery was against the law and also where they could aid escaped slaves. Between 1830 and the Civil War, the "Underground Railroad" came into being and was well "conducted" by hundreds, if not thousands, of brave Quaker men, women, and children. Levi Coffin, a member of New Garden and one of the Friends who moved to Indiana, is thought to have been the "father of the Underground Railroad." He was ably assisted by his cousin Vestal, Richard Mendenhall, George Mendenhall, Charles Beard, and hundreds of others who kept their affiliation a secret.

Quakers at New Garden, Deep River, and Jamestown dedicated themselves to hiding slaves and "conducting" them safely to Ohio and Indiana, where former members of these meetings helped them become established in free states or assisted them to Canada. While waiting for a way to escape to Indiana, slaves who had seemingly disappeared hid in the woods surrounding the meeting houses as well as in the attics of individual homes. Richard Mendenhall hid slaves in his house, his barn, and in his woods. David Beard was known to have hidden slaves in stacks of animal pelts that he kept in his hat shop. Many

This wagon was used to transport slaves to freedom in Ohio and Indiana. The false bottom held as many as eight slaves. (Photo by Burke Salsi.)

slaveowners approached Quaker homes demanding their slaves be returned. There are stories about the methods used in convincing angry owners that slaves were not there, including plying them with drink, sitting them down to a family dinner, or enjoining them in a game of cards, all while an escapee could be hiding under the floorboards or in the rafters.

For example, the Mendenhall Plantation in Jamestown has a special wagon on display. A panel behind the driver's seat hides a secret compartment where slaves hid on their long ride to Indiana. Farm products were loaded in the shallow wagon bed to hide the alterations. Brave Quaker teenage boys generally drove the wagon of goods and escaping slaves to Indiana or Ohio, as they created less suspicion than adult males. Quakers involved in the Underground Railroad risked everything, including their lives and livelihood in assisting slaves to freedom.

Quakers remaining in Guilford County set out to change the laws of the state by using Manumission Society sympathizers to vote against pro-slavery politicians and abolish slavery through electing anti-slavery advocates into the legislature. Through the revision of the North Carolina Constitution in 1835, which provided for the redistribution of seats in the general assembly, the western part of the state, which was largely antislavery, finally achieved a fair representation in the general assembly. The new constitution provided that the governor and members of the House of Commons were to be elected by all adult white male taxpayers; to vote for a senator, one had to own 50 acres of land. The property qualification had to be removed before the Quakers had a chance of swaying public opinion. In 1857, that handicap was overcome, and many historians believe that a policy of peaceful abolition may have become possible had not the Civil War intervened.

Many non-Quaker families left the state because of their need for more land. Methods of clearing the land and rotating crops exhausted the soil. The important crops of corn, wheat, cotton, and tobacco grew best on new land. Even in the early 1800s, men understood the importance of maintaining the fertility of the fields. The constant clearing contributed to large areas of eroded land. Farmers constantly cleared new ground, for they needed vast acreage to continue the process. Lack of affordable new land caused many farmers to seek land elsewhere.

During the westward migration, the population of Guilford County should have experienced a larger decrease; however, natural increase contributed to some stability of numbers. It was not unusual for families to have ten surviving children, and of those, most married very young. It is also thought that children in the piedmont had a better chance of surviving to adulthood because of the temperate climate, the abundant food supply, and the lack of swamplands harboring diseases. The Revolutionary War and the question of slavery almost put a stop to Quakers moving to Guilford County, yet there was still immigration from individuals of all religions looking for opportunity.

Daily life in these decades between 1790 and 1830 was basically stable and unchanging. Almost everyone was engaged in farming, but many did work "on the side." The census for 1810 reported that 148,400 yards of cloth had been woven and 69,000 gallons of whiskey had been distilled during a one-year period. Other products included hides, gunpowder, and 1,600 gallons of flaxseed oil. The Quakers were particularly versatile and many farmers practiced a craft. As soon as the Quaker sons were of age, they learned a trade from a local businessman or artisan or were sent north to live with relatives to learn a trade. George C. Mendenhall was sent north at the age of 15 by his father to acquire the skills of a tanner. He returned home at 19 and opened a tannery, which stayed in business even after his death.

George Mendenhall became the owner of the house that his father, James Mendenhall, had built. The Salisbury Road passed between his house and the mill. When travelers began requesting refreshment, George started keeping an inn. Legends are told about the tavern keeper in High Point who, being upset at Mendenhall for cutting into his business, convinced the surveyors of a new road to bypass the Mendenhall house. Mendenhall refused to be cut off and bought the land between his property and the new road. He made the road the main street of the fledgling village, which grew up to be called Jamestown in honor of George's father, James, the first settler in the area. There are those who dispute the story, yet it is true that Jamestown was named for James Mendenhall, the first settler in the area.

The increased productivity of the piedmont farms provided enough surplus crops for farmers to sell. This gradually lifted Guilford Countians from a subsistence society. It became increasingly obvious that without waterways to facilitate transportation that the county also needed to attract diverse industry and establish reliable and economical transportation for produce and products. Between 1830 and the 1840s, transportation debates raged in and out of the legislature. It was inevitable; Guilford County had to have modes and methods to transport its goods and people in order to continue its development and growth.

4. The Coming of the Railroad

Even after 100 years of settlement and growth in Guilford County, there was no reliable connection between the eastern towns and the towns to the west. Complaints were aired through the weekly newspaper, through political debate, and in polite conversation. Transportation and commerce were prevailing issues and were on the minds of Guilfordians for a number of years before the problems were solved. Prominent citizens, among them John Motley Morehead, fervently believed that a railroad across the state would eliminate feelings of sectionalism, would provide transportation needed for commerce, and would eventually equate to prosperity by providing opportunities for citizens.

Controversy stemmed from progress Greensboro achieved in the 1820s. Development as a courthouse town brought about the development of major roads radiating into Virginia, Raleigh, Fayetteville, Asheville, Salisbury, and Salem. Indian paths and livestock paths were widened and extended for stagecoach roads to transport mail, people, and goods, and for farmers to purchase goods and sell their farm products in town. Greensboro became a center for trade, politics, entertainment, and the doctor. Jamestown was not far behind with its shops, mills, and location on the route to Lexington, Salem, and Salisbury.

The transportation problem festered for decades. It finally became obvious that without transportation, North Carolina, and certainly Guilford County, would remain a backwoods country. In 1835, citizens of Raleigh obtained a charter and raised subscriptions to build a railroad from Raleigh to Weldon to connect with the Richmond and Petersburg Railroad. With some funding from the legislature, the 161-mile road was completed and proved to be a boon to the prosperity of the state capital. With this success, a 14-year debate was begun between politicians and businessmen. The people in the western part of the state clamored for a rail connection. Many politicians felt "it was too early to tell" and some felt it might be an expensive fad. Others expressed that it would be impractical, too expensive, and too revolutionary. To the despair of the supporters, a "wait and see" attitude was adopted by the state legislature.

In 1829, there were five stores in Greensboro, and the county's first newspaper, the *Greensborough Patriot*, had been published since 1821, although archival issues were not kept until 1826. It was not until 1829, when William Swaim, a self-taught journalist who grew up in Guilford, became editor, that the paper developed a substantial following and reached a high level of prestige. Swaim was insightful, articulate, outspoken, and

Lyndon Swaim, the newspaper editor, also served as an architect in Greensboro later in his career. This Gothic-Revival cottage at 113 Church Street was designed by Swaim. (Courtesy Greensboro Historical Museum.)

supportive of the county. He had definite ideas about modernizing the state and was interested in progress. He promoted the railroad, education, and industry. He was admired and accepted into the highest circles of politicians and businessmen.

The *Patriot* was one of several mastheads that appeared over 50 years. From the beginning, the paper was a sophisticated tome of local, national, and international news. Sections captioned "departments" featured literature, poetry, announcements about inventions, new laws, and articles about people breaking the law. Publication of a newspaper in Greensboro has been virtually non-stop through the present day, with the exception of small interruptions between ownership and a long period during the Civil War when there was no paper and no labor to set the type and run the press.

William Swaim died in 1835 at the age of 33. The paper changed hands twice in three years, and Lyndon Swaim, a former newspaper assistant and distant cousin of William, purchased the paper. He was joined by a partner, and they re-established the newspaper into a position of prominence in the state.

Small industry developed. Businesses like the Pioneer Foundry made metal plows and tools. There was competition in the discovery and development of labor-saving inventions, as well as an all-out Greensboro eagerness to attract greater commerce to the area. One issue of the *Patriot* in 1826 headlined, "Labor Saving Inventions." The article reported several inventions by local citizens, including a hand gristmill created by Moses Mendenhall, and it stated, "This mill may prove very serviceable to the southern and western states, as it can, at a very trifling expense, be attached to a cotton gin or other machinery; it grinds by hand, nearly as fast as the water mills with four feet stones. Mr. Mendenhall, the inventor, possesses considerable mechanical genius." The same issue described Benjamin Overman's invention of a sawmill to go by hand, "for sawing straight or circular timber for coach makers." Overman and John Russell invented a machine for cutting off fur as well as a loom for "weaving plain, double, or figured cloth." On

In 1830, Henry Humprheys was the richest main in Greensboro. He built a massive three-story house on the corner of Elm and Market Streets, which became known as "Humphreys Folly." Through the years, it also served as a store, pharmacy (as seen here in 1959), hotel, and the first location of the Keeley Institute. (Courtesy Greensboro Historical Museum.)

Wednesday, August 9, 1826, the *Patriot* announced, "Mr. Herman Allen of Randolph has constructed a planing machine which will perform the labor of twenty men with hand planes. The machine is to be put into operation by water or horsepower and the cost will be but a trifling."

In this atmosphere of development, Henry Humphreys left his saddle and harness business in Jamestown and moved to Greensboro to build the Mount Hecla Mill, the first major industry in the county. It was the first cotton mill in North Carolina and the first cotton mill to be run by steam in the South. By 1832, it was operating on the corner of Bell Meade and Green Streets in Greensboro. It produced woven cotton material and cotton yarn. When the mill was first established, the yarns were so popular that people from the country camped all around the factory, waiting for the yarns to be produced. Yarns and fabrics were hauled in large wagons to Virginia, Tennessee, Kentucky, and Western North Carolina.

Building the facility was a massive undertaking. The machinery was hauled overland from Petersburg, Virginia, and from ships unloading at Wilmington. James Danforth came from Paterson, New Jersey, to set up the machinery and spent a year teaching the white mill hands how to run it. The four-story brick building was 150 feet long by 50 feet wide. Approximately 2,500 spindles and 75 looms were run, and sheeting and shirting were woven. Cotton yarns were put up in 5-pound packages and sold to homemakers to be woven on old-fashioned looms.

In 1837, Humphreys printed and issued his own currency to pay his mill workers. The certificates featured a picture of the Mount Hecla Steam Cotton Mill. The 50¢, $1, and $3 paper bills were made payable to Thomas R. Tate, Humphreys's son-in-law. Humphreys became Greensboro's wealthiest citizen and built the largest house in town.

His three-story house on the Courthouse Square was known as "Humphreys' Folly." By the 1850s, Humphreys found that he needed greater water pressure to run his mill and relocated it on the Catawba River.

John Motley Morehead and William A. Graham, of Hillsborough, spearheaded the movement for a state-supported railway system. Morehead and his brother, James T., married sisters and settled in Greensboro prior to 1827 to establish a joint law practice near the courthouse. Morehead established a business, purchased a house, and won an election to represent the county in the state legislature. He set a pace that led him to become the leading politician and businessman of his times.

John M. Morehead was a multi-faceted, brilliant individual. He studied with Dr. David Caldwell before graduating from the University of North Carolina. He acquired vast land holdings in Guilford County and in Eastern North Carolina, particularly in Carteret County on the coast, where Morehead City was named in his honor. In addition to his law practice, he was an expert in practical surveying and well informed on mechanics and agriculture. He also started other businesses and was active in establishing a bank, an insurance company, and a seminary for young women in Greensboro. On December 22, 1827, he posted the following notice in the *Patriot and Greensborough Palladium*:

> I shall be at home during the month of January 1828. I wish those who are indebted to me on open account to close them by that time with cash; if they are not closed by cash or bonds well secured, I shall bring suit; those indebted

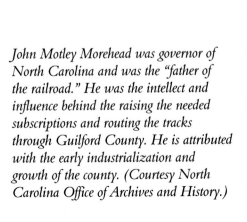

John Motley Morehead was governor of North Carolina and was the "father of the railroad." He was the intellect and influence behind the raising the needed subscriptions and routing the tracks through Guilford County. He is attributed with the early industrialization and growth of the county. (Courtesy North Carolina Office of Archives and History.)

by bond must make immediate payment, or their bonds must be well secured. I must have some money; and my continued engagements from home require that my outstanding debts should be well secured. I give this timely notice to avoid complaint. Stills for sale; repairing of stills will be done at any time.

When he became governor in 1840, Morehead made the building of a railroad, education, and asylums for the insane the cornerstones of his platform. He was disappointed when his best efforts could not get a railroad charter approved during either of his two terms (two years each). He returned to Greensboro in 1845. He remained the most influential man in the state and his home, Blandwood, was a center for political and social affairs until his death.

In the 1840s, the land that became High Point was a minor crossroads. The area was crossed by the Salisbury Road, which connected to Petersburg, Virginia, and to Salisbury, North Carolina. The close settlement of Jamestown had an inn owned by the Mendenhalls, several mills, a hat shop, a tannery, and a store, as well as businesses of other craftsmen.

Many people felt that the construction of plank roads was the answer to the transportation problem because it was faster and easier to build and was much less expensive to construct. After retiring from the governor's office, Morehead lobbied extensively and tirelessly to convince the legislature to pass a railroad bill. The charter was finally approved in 1849 by only one vote. In the same session, the legislature approved the Fayetteville and Western Plank Road. The ultimate construction of both the plank

Investors of the plank road felt that it would solve all of the transportation problems in North Carolina. (Courtesy North Carolina Office of Archives and History.)

road and the railroad was made possible when partnerships were established between the state government and private investors who purchased stock. This plan enhanced the development of the entire county.

The competition between the railroad supporters and the plank road supporters was eased in Guilford County when the Fayetteville and Western Plank Roads were constructed to intersect with the railroad. Both the plank highway and railroad encouraged the expansion of existing villages, and were instrumental in the establishment of new settlements. The town of High Point, in southwestern Guilford County, was literally created at such an intersection. The route of the plank road became High Point's Main Street; the same one used today.

The land for the railroad project was surveyed in sections, with the third section stretching from the eastern Guilford County line to Lexington in Davidson County. The supervisor of the third section, Captain J.L. Gregg, found that his section would intersect at the highest point of land in the area, at 916 feet above sea level. He proclaimed the spot, "the high point," and the village that grew up at the crossroads was thus appropriately named. When the survey indicated that the tracks would intersect with the existing plank road, speculators rushed to buy land at what they hoped would be the crossing.

The construction of the plank road began immediately after the approval by the legislature. The charter stated that the road must not be less than 10 or more than 30 feet in width with a 100-foot right-of-way. Because of the abundance of forest growing all along the route, timber was easily accessible. Since sawmills were transported to the construction sites, oak and pine were milled on the spot. Pine was chosen for the lower part of the road and oak for the upper. Depending on the weather, 15 men could lay a mile of road in about five days. The road had a 3-inch oak plank surface that gave it the name "plank road." It was constructed on a base of pine logs, and upon completion, it was 129 miles long. It was the longest plank road ever built and was often referred to as the "Appian Way of North Carolina."

Stagecoaches, buggies, and horse-drawn carts benefited from the plank roads. Stagecoach companies set up reliable schedules. Farmers had confidence their produce would get to market without spoiling. Henry C. Davis, a young African American, became a well-known driver on the Salem to High Point route. He cut a dashing figure in his fine high boots, tailcoat, and his high beaver hat. He would blow three blasts on his bugle to let people know that the stagecoach was approaching the Jarrell Hotel in High Point across from the railroad depot.

The influence of the road upon the manners and customs of the people was striking and interesting. They were able to send produce, their dried fruit, beeswax, and other commodities to the markets. An old driver remarked, "people began to put on airs, dress better, move their pig pens back of their houses, fix up their homes, yards and garden, grease their boots and harness, curry their horses and to quit using the old accustomed designation 'meat sop' and call it 'gravy.' "[1]

Each day, about 60 vehicles were on the road, which was only wide enough for one wagon; the vehicles bound for market had the right of way. A series of tollhouses were set up at intervals to collect revenue to repay the construction debt and return a profit to the investors. Conveyances entering the road were required to stop at the nearest tollhouse;

anyone caught avoiding tolls was fined. Many local folks rode up and down the road between tollhouses as a diversion; they would enter the road and then turn around before reaching the tollhouse.

Inns along the way served food and provided overnight accommodations, especially for stagecoach riders. Many who provided their own transportation and those who could not afford an inn would camp along side the road. Regular camp-type areas became established near tollhouses. At night, travelers gathered around open fires to cook, to warm themselves, and to share stories. The next morning, they would be ready to leave as soon as the toll operator lifted the gate and collected the toll.

In 1850, there were five inns and a diversity of commerce in Greensboro. W.C. Porter opened a drugstore, Andrew Weatherly operated a dry goods shop, E.W. Ogburn sold books, R.G. Lindsay ran a hardware store, and T.M. Woodburn made confections. The general stores were run by John L. Hendrix, W.W. Gilmer, and John M. Logan. There were also businessmen Rankin and McLean, McAdoo and Scott, James M. Hughes (a tailor), and A.P. Eckels (a jeweler). Other businesses included manufacturers of silk hats, carriages, tannery with a harness and saddle shop, a furniture plant, and shoe factory. The *Greensborough Patriot* was patronized by many businesses advertising their wares. Local newspaper editions from 1826 to 1860 featured advertisements for doctors, dentists, tanners, hat makers, importers, piano salesmen, sewing machine companies, still repairers, buggy makers, carpenters, and booksellers.

By 1850, the money for the railroad was raised, with John Motley Morehead acquiring two-thirds of the funds from private investors. At the stockholders meeting in July 1850, John Motley Morehead was elected president of the railroad company and the stockholders voted him a salary of $2,500 per year, which was thought to be an exorbitant amount. However, it took until June 25, 1851, for most of the construction contracts to be awarded. The *Greensboro Patriot* in 1851 published a letter from the assistant engineer on the second division of the North Carolina Railroad, and the editor of the paper introduced the letter with the following:

> It is with a peculiar feeling of satisfaction that we introduce to our readers the following letter from the assistant Engineer on the second division of the North Carolina Railroad. The success in the letting of contracts so far exceeds our expectations as to dissipate any lingering doubt of the ultimate success of the work. We shall soon have tangible evidence of the wonders which union and determination can effect for our State. North Carolinians can work every where else—build up names for themselves, and character for other adopted States: we shall now see what they can do at home.

The letter from engineer James C. McRae on June 25, 1851, from Hillsboro appeared as follows:

> Messrs. Editors: Doubtless your community would like to know how contracts for grading the North Carolina railroad progress. Having been with the President and Chief Engineer on the whole route, I will make a brief statement.

Contracts were taken readily at Goldsboro for grading the whole track to the Johnston line, except one section of about half a mile.

On Saturday last the lettings were at Pineville; the residence of Dr. Josiah O. Watson, that whole souled railroad man and hospitable gentleman. He submitted a proposition to take at once the Bridge across Neuse and all the Road, which his neighbors did not wish to take, from that river to the Wayne line; and by way of showing his confidence in and liberality towards the Road, he proposed to take it all in stock. This is the gentleman who first proposed that he would be one of a hundred to build the Road. Indeed, a half dozen such noble spirits could do it.

At Raleigh the whole Road was let from Neuse to the Orange line, except two sections. Today the whole route was let from the Orange line to a point some five miles west of Hillsboro.

Thus, you will perceive that the whole Road is under contract from Goldsboro to five miles beyond Hillsboro except these small sections; and contracts were readily taken one half in cash, the other half in stock of the Road and the other contracts below Raleigh are to be completed by January 1853.

At Raleigh the citizens had a most uproarious meeting, an account of which doubtless you will see in the papers. They recommend that ground should be broken in your town on the 11th of July next at the meeting of the Stockholders and that the President invite distinguished strangers to be present on the occasion,—which was forthwith done.

John Motley Morehead's dream was to have the North Carolina Railroad cross the state. The train is pictured here crossing the Neuse River in Craven County on its way to Guilford County. (Courtesy North Carolina Office of Archives and History.)

The meeting was held in Greensboro on July 11, 1851. There was much oration, the driving of the first spike, barbecue, celebration, and most importantly, there was great excitement and expectation among the citizens. The *Greensborough Patriot* of July 12, 1851, reported that "a crowd of people appeared, ready for a celebration." They reiterated that the town had never seen such crowds. The editor described the excitement as follows:

> The procession was formed with the clergy in front; then the stockholders; then the orders of Odd Fellows and Free Masons, who turned out in great numbers and in full regalia; closing with the citizens. This immense line moved down South Street to a point on the Railroad survey nearly opposite the Caldwell Institute building, where a space of a hundred feet each way was enclosed by a line and reserved for the ceremony of the day. The north side of this space was occupied by the ladies, whose smiles are always ready for the encouragement of every good work and word. The other three sides were soon occupied by the male portion of the assemblage, from ten to twenty deep all around.

The *Patriot* reported that Morehead delivered a speech introducing the Honorable Calvin Graves. His address alluded "to the necessity so long felt by our people for an outlet to the commercial world and to the inception of a great scheme the commencement of which we have met today to celebrate." He praised Calvin Graves as the speaker of the Senate who delivered the deciding vote in favor of the railroad. The editor of the *Patriot* was a proponent of the future of the railroad and took the opportunity to comment on the President of the United States in the July article:

> The President of the Republic lately assisted in celebrating the completion of a great northern railroad; we do not see why he might not with equal propriety participate in celebrating the beginning of a southern road, equally great in proportion to the population and resources of the section where it is located, and promising equal importance as one of the strong links of our Union. We hope all events to have the Governor of our own good old State: to none will the freedom and hospitalities of our town be more cordially tendered, on account not only of his official station, but of the estimate in which his amiable character as a man is held among his old acquaintances.

Track laying began at the western terminus at Charlotte and the eastern terminus at Goldsboro and was laid in the direction of Greensboro.

Awarding contracts and surveying the final route of the railroad were highly political. In Jamestown, there were opponents who objected to the noise, soot, and smoke. These concerned citizens basically felt it unnatural that humans would be traveling at a speed of 10 or 15 miles per hour and feared both deaths to humans and to livestock that might wander onto the tracks. Irate citizens objecting to having surveyors cross their property caused rerouting. Because of such objections, the roadbed through Jamestown veered to the south, almost a mile away from the original plans. This alteration created additional growth in the Jamestown area with the settlement of the land close to the railroad. It created an area referred to as "New Jamestown."

Joseph Gibson, Andrew's son, was responsible for the grading of the roadbeds for the railroad as it entered Guilford County near Gibsonville. The citizens in the communities through which it passed usually performed the roadbed work. Gibson contracted with the state to work and grade 3.5 miles of roadbed on both sides of the county line for the sum of $4 per mile. Slaves owned by Joseph did the bulk of the work. The roadbed was begun in 1851; the building of the depot was in 1854; and the first train entered the Gibsonville station on October 9, 1855.

When the railroad was completed to Raleigh, the news was brought to Greensboro by a stagecoach driver. The plank road was reached on November 22, 1855. On December 14, 1855, the first engine entered Greensboro on the newly constructed tracks, and a few days later, a celebration was held with John Motley Morehead delivering a speech. However, it was not until January 29, 1856, that the railroad officially opened with a great celebration following the last spike being driven by State Representative D. Frank Caldwell near Jamestown. When the work was finished, everyone loaded into train cars with two engines pulling cheering workers to Greensboro for a celebration. Two trains met in Greensboro; one left Goldsboro in the east and passed through Raleigh and Hillsboro to Greensboro; the second train left Charlotte and arrived face to face with the Goldsboro train. Many citizens came out to greet the men and afterward they returned to Jamestown. The *Patriot* reported, "Yes, the North Carolina railroad is completed and trains are running from end to end, uniting east and west with an iron band that cannot be broken."

The first train pulled into the new railroad station in High Point on November 22, 1855. The station is seen here c. 1920. (Courtesy North Carolina Office of Archives and History.)

On February 1, 1856, the *Patriot* published the first train schedule. Trains left Goldsboro at 2:10 a.m. and arrived at Charlotte at 6:04 p.m. Trains leaving Charlotte at 5:00 p.m. arrived at Goldsboro at 8:48 a.m.

With the success of the North Carolina Railroad and the earlier Wilmington and Raleigh Railroads, Morehead was anxious to continue laying roads to ensure a successful future for the state. In 1858, the North Carolina Railroad was linked from Goldsboro to Morehead City by way of New Bern. After the Civil War, the railroad was laid on a bridge over Gallant's Channel and finally linked Morehead City to Beaufort.

Morehead pushed the legislature to link Greensboro with Danville, Virginia, and therefore link with the Richmond and Danville, Virginia Railroad. The legislature was not in favor of spending additional money; they feared that too much North Carolina commerce would leave the state. This link was not laid until 1861, when Jefferson Davis realized that by laying this 40 miles of rail, it would give the Confederate States of America an internal link to all the states.

After the railroad was inaugurated in 1856, the plank road was reduced to connecting communities with the railroad. By 1862, the road fell into disrepair and the tollhouses began closing. The company sold the road for $750 in Confederate money.

The mid-1800s brought a great concern for the development of industry to sustain the area. Guilfordians were delighted in the 1840s and 1850s when tobacco grown on the local farms became a promising cash crop. Reuben Dick opened a cigar, snuff, and plug tobacco factory, taking advantage of putting manufacturing and transportation near the point of harvest. Just as tobacco was turning into cash, the Civil War interrupted all farming and industry.

In 1851, the Bank of Cape Fear in Wilmington established a branch in Greensboro, and Jesse H. Lindsay was named the cashier. Greensborough Mutual Life Insurance was

The railroad was everything to the development of Greensboro, High Point, and Gibsonville. The first train arrived in Greensboro on January 29, 1856. By 1891, there were 60 trains a day passing through downtown, and this caused Greensboro to be known as "the Gate City." (Courtesy Greensboro Historical Museum.)

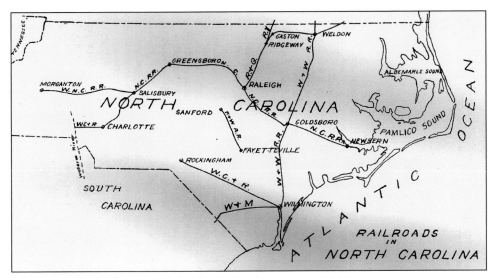

This sketch details the railroads in North Carolina prior to 1860.

also chartered in 1851, and in 1852, Greensborough Mutual Fire Insurance Company was established. Ralph Gorrell, grandson of the landowner who sold the original Greensboro property, became the president of the insurance company, and Lyndon Swaim, the newspaper editor, was named vice president. In 1859, the Farmers Bank of North Carolina opened a Greensboro branch. All of these institutions went out of business during the Civil War.

After decades of diligently building businesses and the creation of a transportation center, it was no accident that the piedmont attracted 80 percent of the industrial plants in North Carolina. In 1860, Guilford had an output of 724,348 pounds of tobacco. The county also listed wood and leather artisans, mills, and gunsmiths as primary businesses and industries.

In 1855, an act was passed calling for an annual election of an intendant of police and four commissioners. In addition to regular duties, the commissioners were required to give names to public streets and were authorized to levy a tax of $1.50 on street lands, $1 a head upon hogs running at large, and $5 upon all dogs save one for each housekeeper. Although many people fed more than one dog, they were careful to claim ownership of only one. There were a number of dogs that belonged to "another family down the street." In other words, a number of well-fed dogs were just "sooners." East and West Streets led into the country. North and South Streets ended after several blocks. The shops were located on East and West Streets, so the name became Market Street; North and South Streets became known as Elm. Other names were chosen to honor outstanding citizens: Greene (for Nathanael Greene), Davie (for William R. Davie), and Gaston (for William Gaston).

In 1858, a new courthouse was constructed in Greensboro on the site of a tavern and near the location of the old structure. It took a year to construct at a cost of $17,383. The *Greensborough Patriot* reported that it was "an elegant and inspiring edifice."

63

This photo was taken of the business section of Gibsonville looking from the depot. This land across from the depot was first donated as a hitching lot.

In 1860, the *Patriot* was sold, and the masthead became the *Times: An Illustrated Southern Family Paper.* It was strongly promoted as a family publication, and new subscribers were enticed by the following statements:

> Many subscribers, heads of families with children, say their experience has been that a good family paper for children is equal to five months schooling. School books give little facts and improving little reading. Newspapers are useful and present practical events of the day. The boy that goes to college and the girl who goes to boarding school needs to be supplied with a good paper.

The *Times* showcased the usual sophisticated features, a children's section, and a column entitled, "Salad for the Solitary." The issues gained popularity for publishing exotic features of foreign countries, especially the numerous articles on China, which covered subjects including the emperor, Chinese religions, and Chinese burial. Novels, published in serial format, helped sell papers. Many readers sought back issues when they realized they were missing serials of excellent novels. This notice appeared in 1860 after back issues were sold out: "Notice that people who were much annoyed by losing the connection of the last story had better subscribe in time. The new story which begins in this issue is 'The Lady of Atherton Hall' by Clara Augusta."

In May 1859, High Point received a state charter. The little settlement at the intersection of the plank road and railroad had 525 citizens, 2 hotels, 2 churches, and 7 stores. The settling of High Point, the growth of Gibsonville, and increased production of farm products including tobacco were results of the North Carolina Railroad. At the same time, the rural western counties gained access to the outside world. By 1859, Greensboro was taking on the appearance of an established town. Public schools were held for ordinary children, and the future seemed brighter with every train that pulled into town.

5. THE IMPACT OF WAR

The ultimate secession of the South from the Union was not popular in North Carolina, and definitely not in Guilford County. John Motley Morehead journeyed to Washington as a commissioner of peace. Although by the time secession actually occurred, there was a display of sectional allegiance by those who simply wanted to show their support for the South. On May 20, 1861, in response to Lincoln's call for 75,000 troops to put down the insurrection in South Carolina, North Carolina seceded from the Union. Because bordering states South Carolina and Virginia seceded, North Carolina had no choice.

Throughout 1860, the editor of the *Times* newspaper in Greensboro faithfully published reports of meetings held and speeches given in states of the North as well as the South. There were "pleas for the Union" and letters discussing all relevant issues including slavery. The April 7, 1860 issue covered the Baltimore Conference and slavery. This issue also featured an editorial commenting on the Southern citizens' objections to Northern literature. As the year wore on, pleas for the Union became more intense, and likewise the Southern states' disdain for Northern oppression was made clear.

The editor of the *Patriot* became increasingly ardent in his editorials that the state should stay in the Union, as can be seen in the following carried in the January 14, 1860 issue:

> Union! The mad foray of a score of reckless fanatics, goaded to their rash act by the ravings of more selfish traitors, continues to be the theme of sectional agitators everywhere. It has hurried us to a crisis that already too surely loomed up in the political future of the Nation. Disunion is discussed on the rostrum, and preached from the pulpit. Disunion is threatened, where once no man dared breathe the word;—its echoes resound through the stately corridors and legislative hall of the National Capitol!
>
> It has found its advocates among the politicians and the press of the North and South—among those whose aspirations are built upon anarchy, and whose ambition can be sated but with blood. The murmurs of dissolution, hitherto too few and feeble, but now assuming so dreadful a significance, have at length aroused the union-loving masses of the people to a sense of the impending horrors. At the North the popular voice has already thundered forth its indignant vindication of the integrity of the Country. . . . it is because our public men have not led the way. The Everetts, the Lincolns, the Cushings, of the

South hesitate to speak out as the champions of the Union. They seem afraid to risk their popularity to preserve that which the Washingtons, the Jeffersons, the Marions, of other days periled their fortunes and their lives to win. We admire the moral courage of the men who in the hot-beds of abolitionism, and in the face of seemingly overwhelming odds, have dared to raise their voices in solemn denunciation of sectional strife, but yet there are none among us to take a similar stand against the fire-eaters of our own section.

By December 1860, a desperate situation was at hand. The December 15th edition printed the future President of the United States' message in full referring "to the present secession movement in the country." An immediate letter to the editor stated that "if the elections were held again, Stephen A. Douglas would win instead of Lincoln." The January 5, 1861 edition carried the following news of South Carolina's secession on December 20, 1860:

Since our last issue before Christmas the times have been eventful. Every day wrought some change in the aspect of affairs complicating the plot of the political drama, drawing it nearer and nearer to a focus, which would inevitably to all appearances, sunder the Union into fragments.

The South Carolina State Convention passed its secession ordinance; the Governor issued his proclamation declaring the state free and independent and the Constitution of the state was amended to allow the Governor to appoint ministers to foreign nations to enter into treatise of peace, amity, and commerce.

A most serious transaction was the step taken by Major Anderson in removing his men from Fort Moultrie to Fort Sumter in Charleston Harbor. In Washington, events have also been exciting. The delegates in Congress from South Carolina resigned on receiving intelligence of the secession of the state.

After the North Carolina legislature received word that South Carolina had seceded, they put a bill before the legislature for appropriating $300,000 towards equipping 10,000 men for army service. The editor stated,

Were we in the legislature we would vote against the bill, first, because there is no necessity for the equipment . . . secondly, there is no money in the treasury to meet the debt of $300,000 after it is made; thirdly, the money might be spent to so much greater advantage for the state in some other enterprise.

The January 19, 1861 issue of the *Times* reflected the desperate feelings of most Guilfordians:

Every day develops more forcibly to our mind the deep seated determination policy of the leaders of the secession to break up the government of the United States. We will not pretend to state their motives, as it is not essential to the question whether these men lead to this course by inordinate ambition to rule, or for fame, or through disappointment, or any other such unworthy motive; but it is fast becoming a fixed fact in our mind that these leaders are totally unworthy of confidence, and it is destruction to follow them.

Subjects of secession, slavery, abolition, and war overflowed into nearly every section of the paper. The selections for the poetry section changed from comfort, spiritual, and tenderness topics to titles including "The Union," and "The Flag." An article entitled "The Crisis" appeared on February 2 with the following statements:

> Our readers may be assured the crisis has reached a point of seriousness which alarms even those who have heretofore looked on with apparent coolness. Whether the Union will be able to survive or whether its days are numbered, no one can tell. We cannot even penetrate into the future one day ahead. It is evident the difficulty must be solved one way or other before the 4th of March. While we hope for the Union with proper guarantees of our rights, we are free to confess the chances are exceedingly slim.
>
> The bigoted spirit of the Pilgrims whose "fathers" we have been accustomed to praise in such unmeasured terms, is still portrayed in its detestable stubbornness exhibited centuries ago. They never yield—but insist on measuring the consciences of others by their self-righteous standard. This being the spirit of the men we have to deal with, we are compelled to fear for the worst.

Governor John Ellis favored North Carolina's secession from the Union. (Courtesy North Carolina Office of Archives and History.)

67

A peace conference was held in Washington on February 4, 1861, as an effort to keep the states in the Upper South in the Union. On the same day as the Washington Peace conference, the already seceded states of South Carolina, Mississippi, Florida, Alabama, Georgia, Louisiana, and Texas were meeting in Montgomery, Alabama, to organize the Confederates States of America. Prior to the meetings, people on both sides of the issue campaigned to win popular support and many meetings were held within 30 counties just in the months of November and December 1860. If one group held a meeting, the other group held a counter-meeting. Zebulon Vance commented that one meeting was "packed as close as herrings in a barrel, by highly excited Union men."

North Carolina sent delegates to both the Union and Confederate meetings. Governor John Ellis, a secessionist, led the delegation to Montgomery, and former governor John Motley Morehead led the delegates in Washington. During the peace meeting, the state of Virginia called for an attempt "to adjust the present unhappy controversies" in a last-ditch effort to win back the seceded states and keep the Union together. During the same period, Congressman John A. Gilmer of Greensboro made strong pleas to Congress urging all states to remain in the Union. Lincoln invited him to become part of the Presidential cabinet.

In February 1861, North Carolinians voted to remain in the Union. Guilford County's vote was 2,771 to 113 against secession. On February 16, 1861, the *Times* editor spoke out against the Confederate states choosing Jefferson Davis as their leader:

> In the first place, we hope our national difficulties will be so arranged as to not only prevent the border states seceding, but also to include the already seceded states to reunite their destinies with the United States of America.

Congressman John A. Gilmer worked closely with Congress and President Abraham Lincoln to avoid war in 1860 to 1861. (Courtesy North Carolina Office of Archives and History.)

If however, this hope is blasted, we lament the selection made by the Southern Congress for a president. General Davis is a brave soldier and might do good service on the field, but in this peculiarly difficult position, we fear he does not possess the calmness and foresight requisite to the performance of the duties imposed upon him.

Following the Montgomery meeting, Governor Ellis returned to Raleigh still favoring secession. The Republicans in Washington were not willing to consider an equitable division of the territories into slave and free areas, and Morehead and the other delegates returned home totally deflated. On March 7, 1861, the *Patriot* published the following:

> Governor Morehead reached home by the Express train on last Saturday night. He found waiting at the station an anxious crowd, desiring to know what had been done, and what was the prospect of peace. . . . Governor Morehead repaired at once to the Court House, which was in a short time, nearly filled. . . . He declined making a speech, but taking a seat on the bench . . . he proceeded . . . to detail what had taken place. . . . The Governor seemed quite sanguine that time would bring all things right, but that if nothing could be done, that the border slave states, together with the border free states, would form a new Constitution for themselves, and take possession of the United States.

There was a change in thinking in April 1861. Congressman John A. Gilmer worked closely with President Abraham Lincoln and Secretary of State W.H. Seward to develop plans to avoid war. Gilmer was assured that Federal troops would be peacefully evacuated from fortifications in states that had already seceded from the Union as a way of continuing negotiations. Instead, the President ordered the resupplying of Fort Sumter—a direct challenge to the new Southern alliance.

When South Carolina heard the news, Confederate troops blasted the fortification, capturing Fort Sumter. In response, Lincoln ordered additional troops to force South Carolina back into the Union. President Lincoln requested that Governor John Ellis send troops from North Carolina. Congressman Gilmer replied to the President, "I can be no party to this wicked violation of the law of the country, and to this war upon the liberties of a free people. You can get no troops from North Carolina."[1]

On April 18, 1861, the *Patriot* ran the following concerning the firing on Fort Sumter in Charleston:

> It is with deep regret and most painful anticipation of the future, that we announce to our readers that the war has commenced. But yesterday, all was quiet, peace and happiness; today terror, excitement, and confusion rule the hour. The Stars and Stripes, the flag which we have been taught to reverence, and which we all so much love . . . has been dishonored, and that, too, by the hands of those, who of all others, should have been the first to defend it.

A few days later, on April 20, 1861, the following comments were carried in the local paper:

> The Old North State did not even call a convention; she will have to secede or become a tributary of the Black Republicans, she will secede it, it is only a matter of time, probably the dilatoriness of the border states will prevent civil war, and it is all for the best; but I should have preferred her immediate secession.

It was ironic that after so many years of lobbying the legislature and having done everything possible to secure a charter to build a rail line to connect Greensboro and Danville, Virginia, that on April 20 it was also announced that a charter had been granted. The following comments from the newspaper illustrate how important the railroad was to Guilford County:

> For many years this whole county has clamored for a charter to build a Railroad from Greensboro to Danville, Virginia, connecting the North Carolina Railroad with the Richmond and Danville Railroad, and forming a direct line of travel North and South. By building this connection, a gap of only fifty miles, there would be almost an air line route, instead of the immense elbow line, heretofore traveled, saving more than fifty miles in distance.
>
> . . . Friends now have a charter offered them and should at once take measures to secure it. To secure the charter it is only necessary to raise in subscriptions, no payment necessary, one hundred thousand dollars. Will the friends of the road do this?
>
> We know the distracted state of the country acts as a great damper upon the public spirit and energy of the people; yet, however destructive and devastating a civil war may be, which now appears so imminent, it should not be an excuse for an entire relaxation from all works of improvement. We should not fold our hands in case, simply upon the probability of the destruction of the labor of our hands, by the devastating scourge of war; or the fearful forebodings that we shall, every man of us, be horribly butchered. We middle-aged men may be killed, but before we die, we can build this road and leave it as a legacy to our children, who will survive and love the land we died to defend. Now we believe this to be a most favorable time to build the road. The tobacco market has been totally destroyed. Our farmers should raise no more tobacco for the next two years, and they will be able to sell the crop now on hand, for as much money as two crops would bring.

On April 27, everything seemed final except for an official vote of secession:

> At present, it is our intention to endeavor to give our readers all the incidents and movements of this great war now going on between the tyrant of the North and the freemen of the South. We may be compelled to curtail the size of the *Times* for a few months, but in doing this, we feel satisfied we have the support and

The State of North Carolina issued currency during the Civil War. The money was worthless during and after the war.

sympathy of our patrons and friends. We will give the same amount of news and will only leave off for a while the literary feature—making the *Times* a chronicle of the times in which we all have taken so active a part. We are reluctantly forced to make this announcement, as two of our printers and the "mailer" are already in active service and the senior editor is one of the 30,000 recently called by the Governor.

North Carolina officially seceded from the Union at a special state convention held on May 20, 1861. When the war began, the county court appropriated $50,000 to equip volunteer units. The citizens mustered a volunteer company, and Company B of the 27th North Carolina became known as the "Guilford Grays." They were initially sent to defend Fort Macon near Morehead City in Eastern North Carolina, and with the fall of the fort, they fought in other battles, including the Battle of New Bern and conflicts across Virginia and Maryland throughout the war. Out of the hundred or so original recruits, only 12 survived to surrender at Appomattox and were paroled.

There were other outfits that organized in the county. The Guilford Dixie Boys became Company M, 21st North Carolina. Abe Jones's grandfather traveled from Bethania in Forsyth County to volunteer for the North Carolina 5th Cavalry because he knew one of the officers. It was usual for volunteers to sign up with friends or at least with people they knew even if it meant traveling to another area.

The towns of High Point and Jamestown became military staging areas and supply points because of their location on two major transport routes. Both freight and passengers increased dramatically on the rail line. Manliff Jarrell, owner of the Laurence House Hotel in High Point, threw up addition after addition trying to keep up with the demand for rooms.

During the first year of the war, North Carolina regiments were trained at a state military facility named Camp Fisher, in honor of Colonel Charles F. Fisher, who was

John Sloan was a captain in the Guilford Grays, a company of volunteer infantrymen who saw action in 20 battles during the Civil War. (Courtesy Greensboro Historical Museum.)

president of the North Carolina Railroad. He was among the first to be killed at the First Battle of Manassas. The camp was located three-fourths of a mile northeast of the train depot in High Point. By November 1861, the camp was abandoned.

The excitement in the beginning of the war quickly dissolved when a severe drought in 1863 and 1864 created a food shortage. Things became even more critical when Confederate-requisitioning parties seized provisions. Enthusiasm for "the Cause" diminished, and peace meetings were held.

In July 1863, a Peace Party was organized in 40 counties, and more than 100 meetings were held throughout the year. On February 10, 1864, William Holden was nominated to run for governor against Zebulon Vance, the popular incumbent. Holden's platform centered on denouncing the war and urging immediate peace by criticizing Confederate policies.

Prior to the Holden nomination, Guilford County held peace meetings beginning on February 1, 1864. Mrs. Jacob Smith attended a meeting with her husband, a minister of First Presbyterian Church, and wrote a report on February 3, which was later published in a pamphlet entitled *The Women of Greensboro, North Carolina, 1861–1865*. She noted, when the opening speech began, that "boys and young men commenced such an awful uproar as was ever heard before, and the speaker sat down." The second speaker was egged, called names, and when he attempted to speak, hymns were sung over his voice. "Mr. Smith says he never imagined such a scene out of bedlam." Scenes like this happened across the state as pro-Confederate advocates drowned out the messages and influence of the Peace Party. Vance was reelected governor, and the Peace Party was abandoned.

The Greensboro and Danville Railroad was built, however, not at the expense of subscribers. The Confederate government realized the need for a valuable inland connection to carry supplies through Virginia, North Carolina, and South Carolina for the aid of troops. Confederate soldiers were directed to build the railroad.

In 1856, Judge Robert P. Dick had built a house he named "Dunleath" on a hundred acres of land near Greensboro. The tracks were surveyed to go right through the Dunleath property. As reparation, the railroad gave Judge Dick the privilege of riding the train free of charge. Judge Dick would flag the train each morning and ride it downtown to his office. A story circulated that one of the soldiers constructing the line became enamored with one of the Dick's daughters, and at her request, he moved the construction over an extra 200 feet from their front door.

The only benefit to the county from the war was the completion of the Piedmont Railroad in 1864, which connected Greensboro to Columbia. It filled in the "missing link" in the track between Columbia, South Carolina, and Danville. The railroad had not been previously constructed because many local politicians and merchants feared that North Carolina products would be filtered out of the state and into Virginia to the north and South Carolina to the south. This unbroken supply line for the Southern troops changed the future of rail traffic through Greensboro. During the remaining months of the Civil War, trains came through Greensboro almost hourly, bearing soldiers and provisions.

There were many tensions created throughout the war. Anxiety heightened after the Federal occupation of New Bern and Beaufort. There was fear that Federal troops might march inland on a mission to destroy the railroad—a major objective of the Federal forces. Gibsonville, High Point, Jamestown, and Greensboro had depots on the North Carolina Railroad—all strategic targets for Union raids.

In the Jamestown area were many gunsmiths. Many of the gunsmiths were Quakers who had manufactured hunting guns prior to the war. Since pacifism is part of their

Left: Governor Alfred M. Scales, from Greensboro, served as a Confederate general during the Civil War. (Courtesy North Carolina Office of Archives and History.)
Right: Junius Irving Scales was Alfred's younger brother, who was wounded five times and imprisoned during the Civil War. After the war, he practiced law with his brother.

religious beliefs, some opted to go out of business rather than have their guns used in warfare. Others accepted contracts from the Confederacy with instructions on how to modify the arms. In 1862, the Oakdale Mill was converted into an arms factory, producing more than 3,000 muskets. The factory still operates today as a cotton mill. Some of the local weapons manufacturers included the Wrights, the Armfields, the Lambs, the Ledbetters, the Stephens, the Counches, the Dixons, and the Johnsons, who had made guns for the Regulators and the soldiers at Battle of Guilford Courthouse. The first guns with percussion locks were made in the county, and "the Guilford Rifle" was well known.

High Point and Greensboro also became sites of arms producers. Tarpley carbines were manufactured in Greensboro. The company originally was Garrett and Company and also manufactured sewing machines. Jere H. Tarpley became a partner in 1863 and registered a patent for a breech-loading carbine. It had two major flaws. First, the gun had no wooden understock to hold; after a few shots, the barrel was too hot to hold. Secondly, the breech did not allow gases to escape, which caused discomfort for the shooter and meant the breech would jam frequently. However, the manufacturer still advertised the gun as "one of the finest rifles on the market."

The county was continually flooded with soldiers. Joseph Wheeler's cavalry and Joseph E. Johnston's army took everything, leaving the citizens barely enough to eat. In the last days of the war, when W.T. Sherman's troops were marching toward Greensboro after the Battle of Bentonville, the commissary stores in McLeansville were destroyed for fear the Yankees would appropriate the supplies. A carload of shells was exploded, and barrel after barrel of molasses and whiskey were burst open. Hungry women dipped up molasses from the gutters in buckets. Thirsty men tried lapping the liquor like dogs.

In addition to rolling bandages and assembling comfort kits for the soldiers, the ladies of Guilford County met trains and took food to share with the troops. Even though there were great shortages of everything, including food, paper, and cloth, families learned to "make do" or "do without." The ladies of the house learned to use substitute ingredients in preparing food. Families valued every comfort they had.

In many cases, women left at home alone with young children while their husbands were away fighting had the responsibilities of taking care of a farm and feeding the family. The poor and average families almost starved. Common necessities were unobtainable unless they could be grown. By 1862, it was almost impossible to purchase food. The prices had risen a thousand times over the pre-war prices. For instance, until well after the war, bacon that had been 33¢ a pound rose to $7.50 per pound. Corn went from a dollar a bushel to $30 a bushel; eggs went from 30¢ to $5 a dozen. Coffee and tea were almost impossible to find, and when they were available, these prized products went for $100 a pound. Parched corn, dried potatoes, and roasted okra seed were substituted for coffee, and Yaupon holly leaves and the leaves of blackberry and raspberry plants were dried and used as a substitute for tea. When the price of salt in Raleigh went to $70 a bushel, the State established public saltworks and provided it at cost.

Shortages were not relegated to food. Everything was scarce, including fabric for clothing, leather for shoes, and paper for printing. Most goods were reserved for the troops. Newspapers could not be published, and wallpaper ripped from rooms became writing paper.

There were no trained nurses in the county, few doctors, and no anesthetics; however, in Gibsonville, Summerfield, High Point, and Greensboro, there were depots. When trains arrived with wounded, they were treated the best way possible. Ladies of the county sewed and quilted constantly. Not even a scrap of fabric was wasted. The tiniest piece of cloth went into a scrap bag, and it was used to make bedding, quilts, and bandages. Everything possible was given for the comfort of the soldiers. The First Presbyterian Church even lowered the bell from their tower and donated it for "the Cause."

Mrs. Jacob Henry Smith, wife of the Presbyterian minister, wrote the following about the ladies who volunteered to meet the trains carrying the wounded:

> Weary, footsore, and needy soldiers were daily passing through the town, who needed to be clothed, fed, and comforted; and whenever the Danville train came in with Graycoats on board it was a signal to broil bacon, bake cornbread, and get out all the milk, buttermilk, and sorghum one could lay hands on, the only delicacies that one could then afford. Sometimes a dozen would file in, occasionally some with unhealed gunshot wounds . . . In this labor of love so freely given for four long years, our women carried a heart-ache that never lifted for husbands, lovers, and friends on the firing line.[2]

It was during the last months of the war that the citizens of Guilford County witnessed devastation in their county. In December 1864, Union General George Stoneman was sent to cut the railroad connections between Virginia and northeast Tennessee. He was also ordered to destroy every factory and confiscate food and valuables as a way of demoralizing the Southerners. He entered North Carolina in March 1865 with 7,000 men and swept through like a tornado. His troops rode across North Carolina, swerved north to Virginia, and then took North Carolina by surprise as troops reentered the state

Reverend Jacob Henry Smith and his wife accepted the call to minister at the First Presbyterian Church in 1859. They worked tirelessly to support their community and "the Cause."

and proceeded to Wilkesboro, Salem, and Salisbury. Stoneman's troops were met with little opposition as they left a trail of looting, rioting, pillaging, and murder. He divided his forces to destroy all the railroads. While Stoneman entered Salem on April 10, he sent Colonel Palmer with a detachment to cut the railroad lines in Greensboro.

Stoneman's Brigade was greeted with white flags as they entered Winston and the neighboring town of Salem. Mayors of both towns immediately surrendered, and the towns were spared excessive harm. One of the members of the local Moravian congregation wrote that "had it not been for the noise of their horses and swords . . . it would have been hardly noticed that so large a number of troops were passing through our streets."[3]

Palmer's men proceeded to Virginia and destroyed the Dan River railroad bridge. Lieutenant Colonel Charles M. Betts of the 15th Pennsylvania Calvary destroyed the bridge and routed the 3rd South Carolina at Buffalo Creek, just 2 miles from Greensboro. Other detachments burned bridges, warehouses, and factories at Jamestown, High Point, the little community of Florence, and throughout the countryside as they marched from objective to objective.

There were over 900 wounded men transported to Guilford County by train after the Confederate loss at the Battle of Bentonville on March 18, 1865. They were treated and "taken in" in High Point, Jamestown, and Greensboro. The enormous stream of wounded pouring into the county forced the creation of makeshift hospitals in every possible location within a 10-mile radius of Greensboro. It also brought smallpox, forcing

Doctor A.J. Sapp was a physician in High Point during the Civil War. At the end of the war, he risked his life to treat soldiers infected with smallpox. (Courtesy High Point Historical Museum.)

Governor Zebulon Vance served as a Confederate officer before being elected governor of North Carolina. As Federal troops descended on Raleigh, Vance fled and set up temporary office in Greensboro. (Courtesy North Carolina Office of Archives and History.)

the operation of a "pest house" on the outskirts of High Point. Fires set by Stoneman's Federal troops threatened the local hospitals. Seventeen hundred bales of cotton were burned by raiders at the High Point railroad depot. By April 11, Palmer rejoined Stoneman at Shallow Ford (near Winston).

When General P.G.T. Beauregard, under General Joseph Johnston's command, left the Battle of Bentonville, he retreated toward Raleigh with refugees fleeing along with his retreating army of 20,000 men. Federal troops were in pursuit and ultimately stopped to occupy Raleigh. Johnston's troops traveled to Greensboro. Governor Zebulon B. Vance also fled Raleigh and set up a temporary office in the law office of Levi and William Scott in Greensboro. When Vance received messages concerning Lee's surrender at Appomattox, he made plans to return to his home in Statesville. After Johnston surrendered at Durham, Vance delivered a proclamation on April 28 and retired.

The war eventually ended at the close of April, but the sick and wounded kept hospitals full for many months afterward. Laura Wesson, a 19-year-old Virginia woman, had been on her way to Charleston, South Carolina, when the Federal army was raiding the county and forced her from the train. She died while nursing soldiers at the "pest house" in High Point. She was buried in a High Point cemetery in the same area where the 50 Confederate soldiers she nursed were buried.

In 1865, in the last days of the war, President of the Confederacy Jefferson Davis escaped with members of his cabinet from Richmond by taking the Piedmont Railroad to Greensboro. Beginning on April 11, and for five days, Greensboro served as a capital of the Confederacy. Davis telegraphed General Joseph E. Johnston and requested a meeting.

The First Presbyterian's small brick church was used as a hospital for Confederate soldiers wounded in the Battle of Bentonville. (Courtesy Greensboro Historical Museum.)

Johnston had been defeated at Bentonville and retreated to Greensboro, where he did meet Davis and discussed terms of surrender. On April 12, he learned of the surrender of Lee at Appomattox.

Johnston's army camped on the land where A&T University was later constructed. The county was overwhelmed with thousands upon thousands of soldiers, including the wounded and dying. The First Presbyterian Church in Greensboro was converted into a hospital, and the dead were buried in the church's cemetery.

While in Greensboro, Johnston delivered the following "farewell" speech to his troops as covered by the March 23, 1866 edition of the *Patriot*:

> We have given up the contest, we have yielded the issue, we have surrendered our arms, we intend to obey the laws of the country, what more can or ought any one ask? We cannot say we are knaves that we are sorry for doing that which we thought right and for which so many of our best men bled and died. We fought a brave fight, we were conquered, we submit. . . . It surely cannot be considered treason to love and revere and honor the names and memories of our noble comrades, friends and brothers who fought and died for the same cause for which we struggled so hard.

Following his stay, President Davis retreated south by wagon because the railroad bridge at Jamestown had been burned. General Johnston proceeded to the Bennett House near Durham and met General Sherman. They agreed on the convention approved by President Davis, but it was rejected in Washington because it undertook to deal with the political status of the seceded states. On April 25, Sherman notified Johnston that the armistice would be terminated in 48 hours. Determined to prevent any further useless sacrifice of life, Johnston met Sherman again at the Bennett House in Orange County, and there surrendered his army on April 26, 1865.

After the surrender at Appomattox and at Durham, more than 39,000 paroles were issued to the Confederate soldiers camped around Greensboro. That was more than twice the number of troops that Johnston had with him during the Battle of Bentonville in March 1865. The paroles were issued over two days, May 1 and 2, 1865. At the time of the war, there were approximately 2,000 residents in Greensboro. While Johnston's troops were in town and coupled with refugees and Federal troops, there were over 80,000 people. The Confederate soldiers departed immediately upon receiving their paroles.

Following Johnston's surrender, the city of Greensboro was occupied by thousands of Federal troops. Judge and Mrs. Dick's house, Dunleath, was occupied by Union General Jacob Cox and soldiers were tented on the grounds. Four United States Army generals—Jacob Cox, Ambrose Burnside, John Scofield, and Judson Kilpatrick—traveled to Blandwood Mansion and were received by former governor John Motley Morehead. One of the generals had brought his wife to stay with him, but the ladies of Greensboro refused to be social.

Union soldiers were camped in yards across the town, and generals selected various properties for their headquarters. Interestingly, Federal soldiers camped on the property where William Sidney Porter lived with his grandmother, aunt, father, and brothers after the death of his mother. Porter later became a famous short-story writer under the name O. Henry. As an adult, he used his memories of the Reconstruction years in several of his works.

Blandwood Mansion was the Morehead home. It was originally constructed as a clapboard farmhouse and was converted into an Italianate villa in 1844. It is listed as a National Historic Landmark and is the oldest example of Italianate architecture in the United States. (Photo by Jim Dollar.)

The Bennett farm near Durham was the site of the surrender between General Johnston and General Sherman. (Courtesy North Carolina Office of Archives and History.)

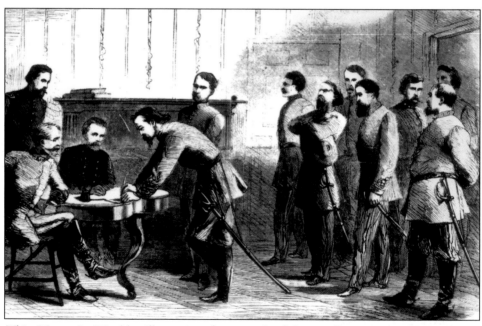

This Harper's Weekly *illustration shows a Confederate officer signing his parole in Greensboro. Officers were paroled in town, enlisted men were discharged by their officers, and then they returned home. The Civil War was over. (Courtesy North Carolina Office of Archives and History.)*

The months of Federal occupation met with few incidences. Citizens and soldiers got along civilly. The immediate problem was that of unemployment for both black and white citizens. The economy was in shambles, and there was desperation in finding enough food and supplies. Letitia Morehead Walker, John Morehead's daughter, wrote the following:

> Wages were paid the Negroes before the troops left the town and their behavior was respectful and creditable.
>
> The philanthropic North sent out agents to purchase lands for homes, churches, and schoolhouses; thus Warnersville sprang into existence. As the farms were well advanced with growing crops, the Negroes remained and received wages and gave no trouble.[4]

After the war, cotton was priced at 60¢ per pound payable in gold, and a suit of clothes brought a thousand dollars. The soldiers who returned to farming wore out their army clothing in the cornfield. Men wore homespun garments and shoes with wooden soles. People practiced every economy that could be imagined. The women who had worked the farms and cared for the family while their husbands were at war continued working beside the men in the fields to get through the period known as Reconstruction.

When the railroad was rebuilt, it helped to revitalize every area that received service. All of the Guilford County stops on the North Carolina Railroad benefited. Greensboro came into its own, for the town was located not only on the North Carolina Railroad, but on the Danville and Greensboro Railroad, an important connection in bringing products and industry to the community.

Members of the United Confederate Veterans (Guilford Camp) held annual reunions following the Civil War, as seen here on May 10, 1928. (Courtesy Farrell Collection, North Carolina Office of Archives and History.)

6. A County Reconstruction

Peace came at a high price; Guilford County and its citizens were destitute. Farms were ravaged by advancing and retreating troops; manufacturing which supported the Confederacy was destroyed. Everything had to be rebuilt to meet the needs of progress. Newspapers throughout the county had been forced out of business and reopened on a limited publishing schedule due to the shortage of ink and paper. Putting food on the table was a struggle. With very little hard currency in circulation and Confederate and North Carolina script valueless, there was no business for shopkeepers. To make matters worse, the state government could not resume—there was a military government in its place.

Plans were laid in July 1865 for the establishment of a police force to take over for the military. All of the freed slaves were placed under agents of the Freedman's Bureau, which was under the authority of Northern soldiers. President Andrew Johnson applied the plan of Reconstruction first to North Carolina. He offered a pardon to all those who took an oath of allegiance to the United States Constitution and promised to obey the laws of Congress. Former senior officers, politicians, and men worth $20,000 had to apply individually. William W. Holden, editor of the Raleigh *Standard*, was appointed the provisional governor.

The Guilford Court of Pleas and Quarter Sessions met on July 4, 1865, and adopted several resolutions. They recognized the authority of the United States Government, pledged patriotism to President Johnson and Governor Holden, and requested the clerk of court transmit a copy of the resolutions to the President and the governor.

Unfortunately, the United States Congress refused to recognize North Carolina for readmission to the Union. It inflicted the Reconstruction Act on March 2, 1867. Instead of moving forward, the state was placed into a military district. It was required to draft a new state constitution for approval by the Congress. A new legislature had to be selected from black and white voters.

Prior to the Civil War, farmers had concentrated on tobacco production hoping to develop a lucrative cash crop. The promise of prosperity dissolved with the war and Reconstruction made recovery a painstaking process. When the farmers left for war, there were only women and children left to plow, till, and harvest. Farmers returning to their farms found devastation, but it could have been worse. Since only one-third of the citizens of Guilford had been slaveowners, most of the families were accustomed to working their own land.

This model farmhouse was constructed by Northern Quakers of the Baltimore Association on Nathan Hunt's land following the Civil War. (Courtesy High Point Historical Museum.)

Quakers in Northern and Midwestern states became aware of the devastating conditions and formed the Baltimore Association in 1865 to launch a program of relief. They focused on providing food and clothing. For seven years, they provided assistance for the repair of homes, buildings, the restoration of meeting houses, and the opening of schools. They created a "model farm" on the Nathan Hunt land in the Springfield community for the purpose of demonstrating and implementing new farming methods to boost the land's productivity.

William A. Sampson of Maine, an expert in scientific farming, directed the agricultural project. In 1868, the best models of farm buildings of the time were erected. There were corncribs, poultry houses, seed barns, sheds for equipment and fertilizer, and a granary. Modern equipment was brought in and included a mowing machine, reaper, horse wheel hay rake, grain drill, clover seed header, and clover huller. A tread mill operated by an ox cut feed, shelled the ground corn, and sawed wood. An old gristmill was converted into a mill for making bone meal for fertilizer. Soil was built up by means of clover, cow peas, and other cover crops.

Friends of the Baltimore Association donated thoroughbred cattle. The farm was also stocked with registered Berkshire and Poland China hogs and a stock of sheep. This experimental program revolutionized farming in Guilford County. After three years, there were 17 agricultural clubs with a membership of 1,500 people, and many local farmers began to subscribe to agricultural papers. By 1871, 1,000 people had visited the experimental farms to witness the new methods, which they adopted for their own farms.

Over 4,500 former slaves started a new life with aid from the Freedman's Bureau sponsored by the federal government. However, more help came from the Baltimore Association. The ravages of war left many people homeless and hungry. Many had no education and nowhere to go. The Quakers assisted with relief and started schools for black children.

Two Quaker ladies arrived in Bruce's Crossroads from Philadelphia on a mission to teach children of freedmen. They used the Peace Church for their classroom, much to the displeasure of some of the local residents. Shortly after the ladies returned home to Philadelphia, they were instrumental in having the Northern Methodists buy the building and donate it to the African-American population. It became the Summerfield Negro United Methodist Church, and the name was later changed to Peace Methodist Church.

Yardley Warner, an agent of the Association of Friends of Philadelphia for the Relief of Colored Freedmen, acquired 35 acres south of Greensboro, divided it into 1-acre tracts, and sold them for reasonable prices. He had a vision for residents to have ownership of a house and land. He established a school for black children in his home and helped freedmen find work in small businesses. In 1867, he organized and built a community school where students, including adults, could learn a trade as well as learn to read and write. Warner returned to Pennsylvania, but the area remained Warnersville and later became the site of three public housing projects.

Many rural farmers delivered produce to residents of Greensboro on Saturdays. (Courtesy University Archives and Manuscripts, Jackson Library, University of North Carolina at Greensboro.)

The rebuilding of the railroads after the Civil War brought commerce to the piedmont. The scene here shows horse-drawn carriages and carts lined up near the railroad station on Greensboro's Elm Street. (Courtesy North Carolina Office of Archives and History.)

A former Union army officer, lawyer, and author, Albion Tourgee came to Guilford County after the war. He was among many new residents who relocated to the piedmont from the North for the warm climate and the possibility of establishing a business. Tourgee started a nursery business and employed freedmen. He was very outspoken about conditions for blacks and former white Union supporters. Even though some citizens labeled him a "carpetbagger," he was elected to be a delegate to North Carolina's constitutional convention in 1868. He also became a judge and was instrumental in the founding of Bennett College.

John Motley Morehead died in 1866, having completed the fulfillment of his dream. He was quoted, "Living, I have spent five years of the best portion of my life in the service of the North Carolina Railroad; dying, my sincerest prayers will be offered up for its prosperity and its success; dead, I wish to be buried along side of it in the bosom of my own beloved Carolina."[1] By 1868, the railroad had been rebuilt, and there was optimism when the City of High Point subscribed $10,000 toward the completion of the Western North Carolina line, which would run through Asheville and into Tennessee. This gave citizens hope for new growth in trade and a reason to attract and establish industry.

In 1873, the Northwestern Railroad Company opened a track to Winston-Salem, and by 1890, it extended to North Wilkesboro. The Cape Fear and Yadkin Valley Railway Company connected in Greensboro to a terminus in Mt. Airy in 1888 and made Greensboro a railroad center with a passenger station and a freight depot. The depot was located at the Davie Street Underpass with trains running in six directions. The railroads gave the state an excellent rail system, but North Carolina was the only state on the Atlantic Seaboard that did not have direct rail lines to the west. Rail lines that ran to

Captain William Henry Snow moved from Massachusetts and is known as one of the first industrialists in the county. (Courtesy High Point Historical Museum.)

the west from Greensboro dead-ended at Murphy on the far mountainous border. The route to Winston-Salem ended in Wilkesboro, and the Atlantic and Yadkin dead-ended at Mt. Airy. Local railroad officers and businessmen proposed, on numerous occasions, track extensions of 50 miles and 80 miles to any of these lines. There was great eagerness to have these plans executed to expand Guilford County as a hub of railroad activity.

With the construction of depots in Summerfield, Gibsonville, Jamestown, and High Point, the entire county developed convenient railway connections. A Western Union office opened in 1870, improving communication and connecting the county to news outside the state.

Aside from the railroad, the greatest advance was the post-war concentration on industry. Businessmen had an eye to attract industrial companies like those in the Northern states. William Henry Snow, a veteran of the Union army from Massachusetts, served in the county during the Federal occupation and became aware of the abundance of forests and the temperate climate. He moved to Greensboro for his wife's health and opened a factory to manufacture shuttle blocks for Northern textile mills. In 1867, he shipped a barrel of shuttle blocks made of persimmon wood to E.A. Thissell in Lowell, Massachusetts. Previously, such products had only been made of apple wood. Snow discovered that persimmon, dogwood, and hickory had value. Men came 10 miles to see Snow, the man who was foolish enough to pay money for dogwood. In 1872, Seborn Perry convinced Snow to move the operation to High Point. This marked the beginning of a competition between the two largest cities in the county and was the beginning of the furniture industry, which caused High Point to develop into a prosperous city.

Author Sallie W. Stockard, a well-respected local historian at the turn of the twentieth century, remembered Snow as being the busiest man in the county for 15 years. He had all of the wood business in High Point under his management. She recalled that things took off from that point and many entrepreneurs came into their own participating in the new-found wood business. J. Elwood Cox purchased Snow's original spokes and handles, shuttle blocks, and bobbins business and increased his productivity until he had established mills throughout North Carolina and sold 90 percent of the shuttle blocks in the world. Cox also helped establish the Globe Home Furniture Company and built the Elwood Hotel.

Seborn Perry built the first steam plant in High Point. The use of steam adapted to industry was a modern marvel compared to hand labor and horse-drawn power. He also built the first residence in High Point on the main road, now known as Main Street. This encouraged other businessmen to purchase lots. Perry acquired two lots with a front of about 84 feet on the Plank Road. The two lots also had a 218-foot front on the railroad.

Although carpetbaggers received a large share of criticism, when it came to the bottom line, they were welcome, for they brought new ideas and money. They brought their business connections and the willingness to take risks. In 1869, Lyndon Swaim, the editor of the *Greensboro Patriot*, sized up the situation in an editorial. He mentioned the skill, money, economy, industry, and willing hands "to join the people in a long pull and a strong pull for the prosperity of a war-wasted land."

The collapse of the Confederacy had also ruined the banks. A new bank did not open until 1869. By 1870, the county was showing signs of recovery and commercial progress. Several old local businesses retooled. In 1869, the Sergeant and McCauley Manufacturing Company took over the Yarborough and Tarpley Foundry to manufacture cooking and heating stoves. The Greensboro business district grew to be four blocks long on South Elm from its intersection with Market to the railroad depot. High Point became an up-and-coming woodworking center, and made great use of their railroad connection, hauling raw materials in and finished products out.

High Point is seen north from the train station c. 1900. A this time, most commercial buildings were within a quarter of a mile from the railroad station. (Courtesy North Carolina Office of Archives and History.)

The *Patriot* was always supportive of Greensboro, "the city." In 1873, the editor said,

> Our town, (city, we beg pardon) of Greensboro is unmistakably growing and
> improving, ever since shortly after the surrender. The event that seemed to
> everybody the abyss of material ruin turned out to be the recuperating point in
> the history of the town. As a trading place, it is evidently in healthy condition.
> The flood of western emigration has just about culminated, we think, and
> the ebb tide is leaving much good life material clinging to the natural soil.
> Manufacturing, especially in woodworking, employing a large class of laborers
> is turning the rich woodlands into pure gain for the community.

An example of the successful Northern immigration to the South, Robert Martin
Douglas moved to Greensboro in 1873 as a United States marshall for North Carolina.
He had served four years as secretary to President Ulysses S. Grant, and then became a
lawyer and Supreme Court justice. His father, Stephen A. Douglas, gained fame debating
Abraham Lincoln and running as a presidential candidate of the split Democratic Party in
1860. The younger Douglas married Judge Robert Dick's daughter, and he remained in
Greensboro to become one of the leaders of the new era of politics and business.

In 1872, a three-story brick courthouse with columns and a bell tower was constructed
on the northwest corner of Elm and Market. It was the fifth County Courthouse. The
fourth was destroyed by fire and with it most of the county records. The 1872 building
was later replaced in 1918.

*The first county courthouse located in Greensboro was constructed in "Courthouse Square" in
the center of the planned village. The "new" courthouse, seen here, was constructed in 1918
using the walls from the 1872 courthouse that had burned.*

An ox cart was acceptable transportation in 1892. The Foust Administration Building on Spring Garden Street can be seen in the background. (Courtesy University Archives and Manuscripts, Jackson Library, University of North Carolina at Greensboro.)

The years that led up to the turn of the twentieth century brought a strong economy and prosperity. New industry required workers. Many people left their farms and moved closer to town in Greensboro, Jamestown, High Point, and Gibsonville. Young men were attracted to towns in search of opportunity. Urban areas were developed, and it became known to the outside world that there were advantages in relocating to Guilford County. By the late 1880s, established businessmen were attempting to attract capitalists to the county. Tours for potential investors were co-sponsored by towns and by the railroad. The *Patriot* published several Booster editions proclaiming the advantages of living in Guilford County.

The success of the years between 1880 and 1915 is due to the hard work of multi-talented visionaries. W.H. Ragan is an example of an ambitious and successful businessman. He was the secretary and treasurer of Eagle Furniture, president of Oakdale Cotton Mill at Jamestown, president of Southern Chair Company, director of the National Bank of High Point, director of the National Bank of Greensboro, director of Wachovia Loan and Trust in Winston, and treasurer of High Point Hardware.

The furniture industry in High Point enjoyed a head start on other commercial towns with the inventions and visions of William H. Snow. Many others followed in Snow's footsteps. In 1902, S.H. Tomlinson began Tomlinson Chair Manufacturing Company. In 1924, Tomlinson and his brother, C.F., built a showroom and office building in High Point and were employers of 900 people. Tomlinson was the first High Point company to show its goods in Northern markets and was the first to use national advertising for marketing. From the beginning, the company trained it own employees, and many skilled craftsmen emerged for the benefit of the entire industry.

In the early 1900s, the Central Carolina Fair sponsored horse racing and harness racing. (Courtesy North Carolina Office of Archives and History.)

Industrial development created a long-term future. Development of the furniture business that Snow envisioned was a natural. There were large forests close to the manufacturing facilities. With the conversion from waterpower to steampower, mills no longer had to be located on the banks of a water source. The county proved to potential investors and clients its advantages over commercial locations in other states.

Sallie Stockard recalled that in 1900, High Point was such a successful industrial center that with a population of 5,000 there was a factory for every 133 inhabitants. She attributed the success of the area to legitimate business and hard work. She stated, "High Point has no 'dead elephants,' no wrangling."[2] She further described the Deep River community as a well-known area of beautiful homes, farms, and one of the very few places in the county that had never had a barroom.

Prosperity gave the population more time and money. A demand for entertainment developed. The Central Carolina Fair was constructed in 1900 on 32 acres a few miles out of Greensboro with two exhibition halls and a half-mile horse-racing track, which featured events of trotting, pacing, running, horse-driven single, double, and tandem, and vehicles drawn by dogs. By 1902, there were displays of farm machinery and exhibits and contests including horses, sheep, cattle, swine, poultry, painting, sewing, embroidery, fruits, vegetables, and flowers. In 1934, the event became known as the Greensboro Fair and later the Greensboro Agricultural Fair. The fair provided excitement for all ages and sponsored events such as speakers and head-line entertainers. In 1954, the horse-racing competitions were changed to automobile-racing contests.

By far, the most exciting celebration in the history of the county was the observance of the 1808–1908 Greensboro centennial. On October 17, 1908, the week-long festivities began with special church services throughout the city, followed by an afternoon sacred concert featuring the United States Marine Band. The city acquired a new Hippodrome building and throughout the week, concerts and speakers were presented. Monday was education day; the U.S. Military Band led a parade of 10,000 schoolchildren and employees. Military Day on Tuesday featured interesting, imposing, and instructive presentations, and Fraternal Day, on Wednesday, told the history of the city. The Thursday concentration was on exhibits at the Central Carolina Fair Grounds, where many people were attracted to a conference on "good roads." Friday was Greensboro Confederate Veterans Day.

People became more mobile and travel by train became part of the culture. For those who could afford leisure time and spend a little money, excursions to Morehead City and other points of interest in the state became popular.

In addition to industrial goods and produce, the train was the mass mover of people. It carried families, vacationers, and businessmen. Prior to becoming the president of

Greensboro celebrated its centennial in 1908. A special arch was constructed to welcome visitors to the city. (Courtesy North Carolina Office of Archives and History.)

the Normal and Industrial College, Charles D. McIver traveled throughout the state on behalf of the Teachers' Assembly. Everywhere he traveled, McIver conducted workshops to help improve the quality of public education. He was a regular train passenger and spent hours studying his books as well as studying mankind. He regularly wrote his wife, Lula, before and after their marriage. All their letters are in the archives of the Jackson Library at the University of North Carolina at Greensboro. The following letter is a look into train travel in the 1880s:

McIvers
General Merchandise
Sanford, N.C. 12/24/1884

My Dear Miss Lula,
(Goldsboro)
I had a very pleasant trip home arriving here at 10:18 last night. I shall take a horse and buggy belonging to the store and go out home directly. "Dunk" was here and staid with me at the hotel last night. He is living by himself now. Mamie, as I told you being away on a visit. Dunk and I will have a time at his house one of these nights. I had a pleasant stay in Raleigh—was invited to tea at three places which was a pleasant indication that my friends had not forgotten me. Tho' I could not or did not accept any of them. I was busy. On my way home from Raleigh I read Dr. Sevier or as Narcisse calls him "Doctah Seveah." My book and my surroundings were very congenial to each other. I went into the smoking car and there as I was reading the few introducing chapters I saw the greatest mixture of humanity—that—I ever saw on a train. Negroes, white-trash, respectable white near drunk, drummers, quacks, and sharpers of every sort nearly. Above the political discussions the said respectable young man in the meantime making a "brilliant and effective" speech for Cleveland for President. I could hear a voice in the opposite end of the car, whose style and dignified accent proclaimed him to be a Negro preacher, reading to an admiring crowd of colored brothers and sisters the 12th Chapter of Ecclesiastes. The conductor passed thro' once and his uniform kindness and politeness to every body and his patience with the aforesaid "Rev. W.M.," when the latter had enquired, "Cap'n where am I going?" and insisted on a reply, charmed me and taught me a lesson too. I was near a colored courting couple and that was the only thing that indicated anything in the crowd that I would fully appreciate or that was in accord with my own feelings. Yes the "universal passion" is not confined to the rich or the poor; the refined or the coarse; the civilized or the savage. With all their faults they love somebody still.

I returned to my seat in the other car and as I was reading about the troubles of the poor in New Orleans, a woman with two little girls aged about 4 and 6 respectively took a seat in front of me, the woman breaking into sobs and the little girls trembling with nervous fright. Upon inquiry it was found that she had started to her husband's funeral, having received a telegram of his death that p.m. She had a ticket to Cameron, which was 18 miles from where her husband died and she had no money to get farther. A gentleman apparently of means gave her a quarter and I gave her some money which she seemed to appreciate and for which she thanked me most heartily insisting on knowing my name. I felt so sorry for her. She appeared to be a very little woman no more than twenty years old. And her husband had been sick since her youngest girl was a baby.

I find the folks here glad to see me. Dunk wanted to know how Miss Lula was. I hope she is well and enjoying her visit. I was sorry that Miss Pattie would not keep Dr. Sevier after becoming so interested in it and especially after I had read 140 pages of it.

Give my kindest regards to her and accept the love of your best friend.
Chas. D. McIver

By the 1890s, Greensboro was the most accessible city of the state. The North Carolina Railroad, the Northwestern North Carolina Railroad, the main line of the Southern Railroad, and the Atlantic and Yadkin Valley Railroad intersected in Greensboro. By 1902, more than 40 trains a day stopped in the town and Greensboro became known as "the Gate City." The same trains passed through other towns within the county; however, they did not always stop. The stations at Bruce's Crossroads (which came to be known as Summerfield), Gibsonville, Jamestown, and High Point benefited in passenger service and freight hauling for their local businesses.

On June 9, 1899, the Southern Railroad depot was constructed in Greensboro on South Elm Street. The three-story building, with a turret, mansard roof, and covered platform to protect passengers from the elements, was a point of pride for all the citizens.

Judge David Schenck led the preservation of the Guilford Battleground. He purchased 30 acres of the battlefield and founded the Guilford Battle Ground Company, and they are pictured, from left to right, as follows: (seated) J.W. Scott, David Schenck, and D.W.C. Benbow; (standing) J.A. Gray and Thomas Keogh.

In 1882, Judge David Schenck, a noteworthy attorney and North Carolina historian, moved to Greensboro from Lincolnton to establish the Greensboro Graded Schools. In 1886, he purchased the part of the grounds that made up the Guilford Courthouse Battleground to preserve the battleground for posterity. At the time, it was an old sedge field of pines and briars.

On May 6, 1887, David Schenck, J.W. Scott, Julius A. Gray, D.W.C. Benbow, and Thomas B. Keogh organized the Guilford Battleground Company. Mrs. McAdoo-King became the only female stockholder. From 1887 to 1917, the group raised money and acquired 125 acres. In 1889, the North Carolina Legislature appropriated $200 to support the battleground, and in 1891, the park became a cemetery for soldiers and patriots.

The Guilford Battleground Company took over where the Greene Monument Association left off in their attempt to erect a monument to honor General Nathanael Greene. They had begun collecting funds in 1857; the Civil War intervened and the money was lost. The Battleground Company launched a campaign to secure Congressional funding for the monument and $30,000 was provided in 1911. Sculptor Francis H. Packer was commissioned, and the work was dedicated on July 3, 1915. The

Greene Monument stands among many other monuments dedicated to the men who fought and died with him.

The battleground became a getaway place for the citizens of the county. Large Fourth of July celebrations were held each year with special trains scheduled from each depot in the county to take citizens to the event, which included a picnic, music, and games. The celebration at the battleground was one of the first holiday traditions established in the county, and it is still observed today.

In 1917, the Battleground Park was taken over by the United States War Department and ultimately by the National Park Service. During the Great Depression, federal funds were used to make improvements in the park, but it was not until 1976 that a visitor's center for interpretation was opened.

The period of Reconstruction began as an ideological and economic struggle. It fortunately resulted in a positive period of growth and a bridge of social and commercial improvements that led citizens into the twentieth century. Educational institutions were reestablished and improved with new facilities and well-educated faculties. It was a time when the welfare of all citizens came under scrutiny. Former slaves found a place in society, and by 1900, males and females, white and black, were afforded a public education.

The Nathanael Greene Monument is the centerpiece of the Guilford Courthouse National Park. (Photo by Burke Salsi.)

95

7. Education and Opportunity

The fight against illiteracy began in colonial times, but at any given time in the early years, only about 100 students were enrolled in private academies. The earliest education for most children was offered by literate parents, who taught the basics at home. Some church groups organized classes for a few months a year. Members raised money and paid a minister or an educated church member to hold classes in a home or in a church building. These schools were a type of subscription school referred to as "old field schools." The Quakers provided the most regular education for their children and led the way in establishing schools.

Dr. David Caldwell also led the way in education in Guilford County for over 50 years. His log school was the first school and served as an academy, a college, and a theological seminary. Among his graduates were doctors, lawyers, members of the legislature, and five future governors. His influence upon and advocacy of Judge Archibald Murphey, John Motley Morehead, and William Paisley helped them to become instrumental leaders in making education available to all children across the state.

Private subscription schools were still in existence after the Civil War through the late 1800s. The best remembered and most famous was Evelina Maria Porter's school in Greensboro. Known as "Miss Lina's," it is most noted for being the school where William Sydney Porter, who was later known as O. Henry, received his education. Miss Lina's school was located next to the Porter home on West Market Street. She was Will Porter's aunt, and after his mother died, Porter lived in the house with her, his father, and his grandmother. Miss Porter gained quite a reputation for being a taskmaster. She stressed the importance of punctuality, truthfulness, and cleanliness. At the morning roll call, students answered, "I was not late, I have not broken the rules, and I washed my teeth this morning."[1]

Some children were bound out to a tradesman to learn a specialized craft. Many people of means had their children learn a trade from a relative or friend, even if it meant sending them to live in another state for a period of time. Sons and daughters of the wealthy attended private academies. Orphaned children of little means were often bound out to a master who would agree to teach the child a craft, such as weaving, coopering, tanning, or carpentry. It was not unusual for them to be bound for a long period of time. Colonial Court Records indicate that many children started younger than age 6 and were bound until age 18.

Dr. Lindsay's office was moved from Scientific Street and now stands on Mendenhall Plantation in historic Jamestown. (Photo by Burke Salsi.)

In the late 1700s and early 1800s, Jamestown was the largest and most prosperous village in Guilford County. Neither Greensboro, High Point, nor Gibsonville had been founded. Interestingly, Jamestown was home to a series of medical schools in the early 1800s. Dr. Madison Lindsay opened his classes for students to "read medicine" around 1825 in his Uncle David Lindsay's house on the corner of Scientific and Federal Streets. His school was the first in the county to be recognized by the North Carolina Medical Society. At the time, students learned medicine through apprenticeships. Dr. Lindsay may have received his training from another uncle, Dr. Joseph Wood. Established medical schools were expensive; however, some of Dr. Lindsay's students "of means" also received advanced training.

By 1833, Dr. Lindsay moved his practice to Greensboro, where he also served as postmaster. His advertisement in the *Greensboro Patriot* on April 10, 1833, listed his specialities as "practice of Physics, Surgery, and Midwifery." Dr. Lindsay's original school is under the care of the Historic Jamestown Society and is now located at the Mendenhall Plantation.

Dr. Shubal Coffin also set up a medical practice in Jamestown. In 1856, one of Coffin's former students used an anesthetic during an operation. This was the first successful use of a general anesthetic in North Carolina.

In the 1820s and 1830s, George C. Mendenhall of Jamestown conducted special schools for slaves. Many Quakers throughout the county conducted schools for their children, other Quaker children, and slaves. In 1830, the legislature passed a law making it illegal to educate slaves. Many of the schools continued in secrecy until some slaveowners complained to authorities and there became a possibility of prosecution. Mendenhall was a Quaker leader, shopowner, legislator, and lawyer. He opened a law school near his

Prominent North Carolinian John Motley Morehead, the father of five daughters, constructed the Edgeworth Female Seminary in 1840 on property next to his home. (Courtesy Greensboro Historical Museum.)

home, which he called "Telmont"; many young men who could not afford to attend a professional college "read law" with Mendenhall. Many of the state's successful attorneys and legislators were Mendenhall graduates, including Judge John Dick.

Judge Archibald D. Murphey, state senator from Orange County between 1812 and 1818, led the fight against illiteracy in North Carolina. He repeatedly recommended methods to meet the educational needs of the white children through a State-supported system of common schools. His ideas of education were considered radical; all of his bills were defeated because the majority of legislators considered education to be the responsibility of the individual. Finally, it was realized that there was no future in having thousands of children grow up in ignorance without a chance for a successful future. William Swaim, editor of the *Patriot*, stated, "The fact is too notorious for concealment, hundreds of young sons of North Carolina are growing up, even to manhood—in point of masculine power—without being able to read."

Private academies for students who could afford to pay were fairly popular. In 1824, the Greensboro Academy was established to prepare young men for admission to the University at Chapel Hill. The course of instruction included writing, arithmetic, English grammar, and geography. Composition and elocution were also presented. The $35 fee per session included room, firewood, washing, and candles.

The *Greensborough Patriot* ran many advertisements for academies between 1824 and 1860 and a few were open only a short time. In 1833, a classical school for males was founded in Greensboro by the Orange Presbytery; however, after a few years, it was moved to Hillsborough. John Motley Morehead, John M. Dick, and John Gilmer immediately secured a charter for the establishment of Greensboro High School.

While the young men were studying in the Caldwell Institute building, the well-connected young ladies were studying at the Edgeworth Seminary, established by John Motley Morehead. Young ladies from throughout the state joined his five daughters. They studied waxwork, shell-work, silk and worsted work, in addition to English, Latin, Greek, mathematics, commerce, and Jewish antiquities. The school closed during the Civil War and was reopened from 1868 to 1871 by David Caldwell's grandson, Dr. J.M.M. Caldwell.

The year 1830 marked a decade of progress and vision for education throughout the state. Most of the religious denominations felt that education was of great importance, and private denominational colleges were founded. Greensboro benefited from plans for two schools of higher learning, the New Garden Boarding School and Greensboro Female College.

New Garden Boarding School was begun in 1830, when the Yearly Meeting of Friends requested a report concerning the status of the education of Quaker children. Committees studied the issues of receiving subscriptions and purchasing land. In 1832, a plan was submitted suggesting the location of the school in New Garden. The school was to be self-sufficient, with a farm, orchard, and dairy. The meeting also voted to select members from area meetings who could be educated to teach. After the first plat of land was purchased, Elihu Coffin donated the adjacent 70 acres, and Friends in England donated $10,000. The school opened on August 1, 1837, with 25 males and 25 female students in attendance. It was the first co-educational college in North Carolina and the second in the United States.

The school suffered financial difficulties in the 1850s, but it remained open with the help of Friend's groups throughout the North and South. The school was the only one

The Quakers played an important role in the reconstruction of Guilford County. The New Garden Boarding School was the only area school that stayed open throughout the Civil War. In 1888, the school became a college, and Lewis Lyndon Hobbs was named the first president. Hobbs is shown here with his son. (Courtesy Quaker Collection, Guilford College.)

Surveying was an important and necessary occupation. Students from John W. Woody's surveying class at Guilford College are pictured here in 1885. (Courtesy Quaker Collection, Guilford College Library.)

in the state to continue classes during the Civil War. While under the direction of Lewis Lyndon Hobbs in 1888, the New Garden Boarding School became Guilford College. As endowments increased over the years, Guilford College has prospered as one of the top private, liberal arts colleges in the Southeast.

In 1838, the Methodist Episcopal Church organized the Greensboro Female College as the first chartered college for women in North Carolina. It opened on West Market Street in 1846 with Reverend Solomon Lea as its president. The *Patriot* regularly published news and special announcements. The issue on February 4, 1860, proclaimed, "The collegiate year beginning on the last Thursday in July and ends on the second Thursday in June. Board including furnished rooms. French, Latin, Greek, oil painting, guitar music or piano, mathematics, literature, vocal music." The school changed its name in 1920 to Greensboro College.

With the election of John Motley Morehead as governor, the Common School System of North Carolina began. The 1839 general assembly enacted a law permitting people to vote on the issue of tax-supported public education. The citizens of Guilford voted in favor, and a school board was created in 1841. Dr. Nereus Mendenhall and Dr. C.H. Wiley, of Guilford County, developed the system, which was a major step forward in the state's internal improvement. Dr. Wiley became the first superintendent of public instruction in North Carolina. He organized the forerunner of the present system of public education, established the first teachers association, and developed the *North Carolina Journal of Education*. Even though the railroad had not been established, Wiley visited every county in the state in the interest of schools on horseback or horse-drawn conveyance.

In 1853, the county had 72 districts, 5,989 children reporting, and 3,545 taught. Schools operated for four and half months a year. The average salary for male teachers was $17 per month, and for female teachers, $14. There were 57 men and 19 women employed as teachers.

The schools were closed during the entire length of the war, and it seemed Wiley's work was lost. Immediately after the Civil War, North Carolina instituted a "free school" system for every county. None were established near towns, so many "subscription" schools were again organized in homes. The schools eventually resumed. R.D.W. Connor, the superintendent of Oxford Graded Schools, wrote about Wiley's work as follows:

> The work of Calvin H. Wiley was essentially that of an originator and organizer. Beginning with practically nothing except opposition as a foundation, he built up by his own power, often unassisted, a flourishing system of efficient schools.
>
> Although the strain of the terrible days following the war broke down the system he had founded, so strongly had he laid the foundation, so well had he builded, so deeply had he instilled into the minds of the people the common school idea, that it proved but a temporary suspension.
>
> With the rescue of the State from the hordes which were sucking her life-blood, came the opportunity to redevelop her resources. Far-sighted statesmen and leaders clearly foresaw that the first essential for development was universal education. Upon the apparent ruins of Wiley's system, they founded our present growing, influential public school system, with many of the improvements which Wiley himself would have adopted had he held the helm. Back of all her wonderful development in other matters as well as in school affairs, lies the solid foundation of Dr. Wiley's 3,488 schools and his trained force of teachers.[2]

In 1851, Oak Ridge Institute was founded in the northwest area of the county as a preparatory school for young men. It opened in 1852 with 50 students and Professor John M. Davis as principal. Students came from six states. When the Civil War began, all but three students volunteered for service. The building burned sometime during the war, yet in 1866, Professor O.C. Hamilton and a new board of trustees began re-establishing the school, which is now Oak Ridge Military Academy.

Greensboro's new charter in 1870 brought the one-room schoolhouse on Lindsay Street into the city limits. That same year, the citizens voted a special tax for the support of public schools. This meant Greensboro was the first town in the state to establish a graded school program. Lindsay Street School expanded in 1876 to offer eight grades. Also in 1876, the first graded school for blacks was opened on Percy Street. In addition to these school programs, Guilford County was also the first county to coordinate a rural school program. High Point schools were established in May 1897. In 1901, a tax was voted for the New Garden Graded School, and educational institutions were also opened in Summerfield, Browns Summit, Pleasant Garden, and Gibsonville. By May 1891, the corporate limits of Greensboro were extended, and in that same year, graded schools were provided for both white and colored children. In 1875, only 100 students attended school. By 1897, there were over 1,500 children—black and white—attending school.

In 1890, George A. Grimsley was elected superintendent of Greensboro's school system at a salary of $1,200. The teachers were paid $30 per month. Grimsley also worked for the creation of public-supported community libraries throughout the state. In 1902, he helped write a bill that was introduced in the legislature by Senator A.M. Scales, stating that towns with more than 1,000 people could establish a public library, maintain it with tax dollars, and operate it as part of the school system. In 1902, Greensboro got its first permanent library, managed by Annie Perry, one of the first trained librarians in the state.

The Whitsett Institute was established by William Thorton Whitsett in southeastern Guilford in a community that later became named Whitsett because of the school. The educational institution was constructed around 1888 within 3 miles of the Gibsonville train station. The little village was considered the perfect location for a school because the area was virtually deserted and there was nothing to tempt the students to waste their time. Students were attracted to the school because the county life reduced the normal expenses of attending school in town. Courses were offered to both males and females. A new building was erected for 329 students, and every modern convenience was employed for school work, library, chapel, society halls, gymnasium, and music.

Bennett College, famed for its pioneering work in health education, was started in 1873 as a day school in an unfinished basement of St. Matthews Methodist Church. In 1875, the North Carolina Conference of the Methodist Episcopal Church purchased 20 acres near Greensboro to build a larger school that would also have dormitories. Lyman Bennett of Troy, New York, donated the funds for the first building and it was named Bennett Hall. The co-educational school was dedicated as Bennett Seminary. The Women's Home Missionary Society of the Methodists Episcopal Church built the Kent Industrial Home for Colored Girls adjacent to the seminary, and it was dedicated on May 2, 1887.

Bennett College for African Americans was established in the basement of a Methodist church in 1873. Seen here c. 1890, the institution later became an all-girls school in 1926. (Courtesy Greensboro Historical Museum.)

North Carolina A&T University was chartered as a college for African Americans in 1891. The main building was constructed using student labor and was built of bricks made on the grounds of the school. (Courtesy Les Seaver-Davis private collection.)

In 1881, Reverend Wilbur Fletcher Steele became the principal. During his eight-year term, the seminary received a charter from the State of North Carolina as Bennett College. Charles H. Moore came to Bennett as a professor of Latin and Greek after he had served local public education by establishing the Percy Street Graded School. Both white and black educators worked hard during the first 50 years to ensure the success of the college's programs.

The Agricultural and Mechanical College for the Colored Race was established by an act of the General Assembly of North Carolina on March 9, 1891. It was temporarily located in Raleigh until the citizens of Greensboro donated 25 acres of land and $8,000 to be used in the construction of buildings. In 1893, the general assembly appropriated $10,000 more to be used for construction. Students assisted in laying the bricks, which were made on the campus. James B. Dudley served as the first president.

At the time of the school's development, 80 percent of the African-American population of the state lived in rural areas and subsisted by agricultural endeavors. Classes were offered in science, agriculture, mechanics, and animal husbandry to increase the chances of African Americans owning successful farms and to give them opportunities to develop, design, and repair farm machinery.

While the graded schools for white and black children were developed almost simultaneously, black students were left behind in 1899, when a separate high school opened for white students in the old St. Agnes Catholic Church building on Forbis Street in Greensboro. The board of education offered public aid to African-American students who wished to attend high school at Bennett until 1926. At that time, Dr. David Jones became president. He discontinued the high school program, and reorganized the school

Schoolchildren in High Point posed for this class portrait in 1917. (Courtesy Harris family private collection.)

as a four-year college for women only. When Bennett closed its high school, the board of education established a standard high school for black students, and the James B. Dudley High School was built in 1929. Great plans were made in the 1920s in Greensboro and High Point for building new schools and expanding the entire educational program; unfortunately, the Great Depression put a hold on the vision.

Beginning in 1882, High Point's subscription schools were partially funded as a "public" gesture. High Point entered the 1890s without a public education system even though subscription schools, private academies, and seminaries were out of date. An outstanding educational program for African-American students was started in High Point in 1867 by Solomon Blair with assistance from the New York Society of Friends. It began as the High Point Normal and Industrial Institute, and by 1890, the demand was too great for the two-room facility. The name was changed to William Penn High School in 1891, when a new school was constructed through donations from local Quakers, the New York Society of Friends, and both local black and white citizens. The school continued to grow and became part of the public school system in 1924. Central High was built as a separate high school for white students in 1927. Both schools became part of the desegregated school system in 1968.

The public graded school began in High Point in 1897 after voters approved a $10,000 school bond. J. Elwood Cox, chairman of the school board, arranged for the school to open in an imposing new residence that he had recently built at the corner of Green and

Main Streets. His wife did not like the house, so the students became the beneficiaries of the structure, which served as a school until 1931. During the next 15 years, schools were established throughout the city.

The debate concerning the education for women raged on for years. Zebulon Vance, former governor of North Carolina, advocated equal education for women as early as 1879. The North Carolina Teacher's Assembly passed resolutions each year, between 1886 and 1891, asking for the establishment of a normal college. In 1890, the North Carolina Farmer's Alliance passed a similar resolution requesting the State to aid in the higher education of females. Finally, in January 1891, Governor Fowler urged the general assembly to establish a college.

North Carolina educator Charles D. McIver felt that the state was a century past due in realizing that "youth" meant young women as well as young men. He pointed out that from one-half to nine-tenths of the money used to employ instructors in higher education for young men was paid by the State and national annual appropriations. He philosophized that if the State paid for nearly all the expenses of a young man's higher education, it ought to do as much for his sister. McIver lectured throughout the state and lobbied the legislature until the State Normal and Industrial College for White Girls was established. Edwin A. Alderman said, "If you educate a man, you educate one person; if you educate a woman, you educate a family."[3]

The act required that the school be located in a place where citizens would furnish the necessary buildings or at least the money sufficient to erect the buildings. Greensboro bid $30,000 through a bond and a 10-acre site that was donated by R.S. Pullen and R.T. Gray of Raleigh. The land was near Moore's Mineral Springs and was thought to be convenient,

Students are seen here after chapel in front of the McIver Building at Women's College c. 1930. (Courtesy University Archives and Manuscripts, Jackson Library, University of North Carolina at Greensboro.)

Charles D. McIver, president of the Normal and Industrial School, is shown here with the first faculty of the school in 1893. (Courtesy University Archives and Manuscripts, Jackson Library, University of North Carolina at Greensboro.)

for students could carry their drinking water in buckets to their rooms. At the board meeting of May 1892, members requested that the City of Greensboro extend Walker Avenue to the college. The board recommended the use of cement plaster in the buildings over lime plaster, for the board believed it more durable and not impaired by water. The board ordered gas lighting in the main building at a cost of $67. They also requested that wires for electric lights be installed for potential future needs.

Once an act was passed by the legislature to create the school, the State wanted the institution to be good enough for any of its citizens and the expenses low enough for all. Section 5 of the act establishing the school stated the following:

> The objects of the Institution shall be (1) to give to young women such education as shall fit them for teaching; (2) to give instruction to young women in drawing, telegraphy, typewriting, stenography, and such other industrial arts as may be suitable to their sex and conducive to their support and usefulness. Tuition shall be free to those who signify their intention to teach upon such conditions as may be prescribed by the Board of Directors.

Anyone receiving free tuition had to declare their intention to teach, at least half as long as they received free tuition, otherwise the student paid full tuition. At first, two years of study was offered, and then in 1902, a four-year program was offered. When the school opened in the fall of 1892, there were 176 students. The first graduation was held in 1893.

Qualifications for admission included being able to analyze any ordinary arithmetical problem, reading any ordinary English page fluently at sight, being able to express thoughts accurately in writing, and being able to answer questions on English, geography, history of the United States, and history of North Carolina. Students had to be at least 16 years old, send an application, which they themselves should write, and have a statement of scholarship and character from their last teachers.

The school's early faculty was comprised of talented and colorful educators. By far, P.P. Claxton was the most popular professor. His good looks were legendary. The girls liked him so much that they applauded when he entered the classroom. In 1911, President Taft appointed Claxton the United States Commissioner of Education. Dr. Anna Gove was brought to the school as the full-time doctor in the infirmary. She served as a doctor in World War I and traveled all over the world. Also, President Charles McIver, the advocate for the school, was known to ride to the station in his horse-drawn surrey to personally meet students.

Expenses for the annual session included tuition for the entire course ($40); board in dormitories (not to exceed $64); laundry (not to exceed $12); physician's fee ($5); book fee ($5); contingent fee ($2); total $128.

The first catalogue recorded the following:

> The institution is fortunately located. To the entire people of the state, Greensboro is the most accessible to North Carolina towns. It is the railroad center of the state. The North Carolina Railroad, North Western, North Carolina Railroad, the main line of the Richmond and Danville Railroad and the Cape Fear and Yadkin Valley Railroad meet at Greensboro. The schedule time to Greensboro from Raleigh, Fayetteville, Durham, Winston-Salem, Mt. Airy, Statesville, Salisbury and Charlotte is from one to four hours.

Charles D. McIver (right) poses with the first graduates of the North Carolina Normal and Industrial School in 1893. (Courtesy North Carolina Office of Archives and History.)

Many citizens had a clear understanding of the pressing need for greater educational opportunities for the African-American children and adults. However, it was not until 1921 that the North Carolina General Assembly gave the task of supervising the state's public schools for blacks to the Division of Negro Education as part of the State Department of Public Instruction. The State continued to maintain totally segregated schools until the 1950s, when the separate-but-equal doctrine in education and public accommodations was overturned in the federal courts, and by 1965, all of the schools in the county were desegregated.

One of Guilford County's most dedicated educators was Charlotte Hawkins Brown. She was the granddaughter of former slaves and was born in Henderson. At a young age, she moved to Massachusetts, where her mother felt the family could find better opportunities, including a better education. Charlotte Brown was a visionary who dedicated her life to the education and improvement of black students. In 1901, at the age of 19, she arrived in Sedalia from Cambridge, Massachusetts, to teach at Bethany Institute, a rural black school sponsored by the American Missionary Association, a religious organization that sponsored many African-American schools in the South after the Civil War. Sedalia was a small, rural community situated between Greensboro and Whitsett in the eastern part of the county. It took its name from the first postmaster, who chose "Sedalia" for the post office because he simply liked the sound of the word.

A few months after her arrival, the Missionary Society decided to close all of their one- and two-room schools. Charlotte Brown returned North and raised money to continue the school. Residents donated land and a blacksmith shop, which was converted into classrooms and a living area. She named her school the Palmer Memorial Institute in

Charlotte Hawkins Brown was the founder of the Palmer Institute, which became known all over the nation and world. (Courtesy North Carolina Office of Archives and History.)

Charlotte Hawkins Brown (back row, center) poses with four of her teachers, who lived at the school. (Courtesy North Carolina Office of Archives and History.)

Charlotte Brown's personal residence was built on the grounds of the Palmer Institute and was painted a bright yellow. It was known locally as the Canary Cottage. (Photo by Jim Dollar.)

This is a classroom building on the grounds of the Palmer Institute, founded by Charlotte Hawkins Brown in Sedalia. (Photo by Jim Dollar.)

memory of her friend, mentor, benefactor, and teacher, Alice Freeman Palmer, the first female president of Wellesley College in Massachusetts.

In order to make it through the first few years, teachers and students ate two meals a day, mostly of corn bread, molasses, peas, and beans. Students had to do a variety of chores, including making beds, laundry, building fires in the stove, and carrying water from the well to the dorm. Brown established both elementary and high school curriculums, and by 1917, the Palmer Institute had grown into four large buildings: two dorms, an Industrial Building, and Memorial Hall, which contained classrooms, offices, and a kitchen. In the 1920s, a junior college program was added.

Charlotte Brown saw the school grow from an institution that emphasized agricultural and industrial programs into one of the best-known preparatory schools for black students in the United States. She served as the president of the institution for more than 50 years, during which time more than 1,000 students graduated. The school closed in the 1960s.

Higher education in the southwest part of the county was expanded when the Methodist Protestant Church established a four-year liberal arts college in High Point. A community effort brought the school to the town with a local campaign raising $100,000 and 60 acres of donated land. Six of the first board members were from High Point. The college, now called High Point University, opened with three buildings in September 1924. The programs were on the verge of success when the Great Depression occurred and affected the institution's financial stability. During World War II, a pre-aviation training detachment was conducted under the Army Air Force, and all improvements were donated to the college after the war.

The 1960s saw great strides in education throughout the county. In 1963, the Greensboro City Schools moved to "the freedom of choice" plan and desegregation of the public schools was underway. By the mid-1960s, all of the schools, staff, and central offices had been desegregated.

Guilford County has held onto its institutions of higher education. The University of North Carolina at Greensboro became the Women's College of the University of North Carolina in 1932 and was generally referred to by the citizens as "Women's College." When men were admitted and the college became co-educational in 1964, the University of North Carolina at Greensboro was created. A&T State College (the former Agricultural and Mechanical College) was upgraded to "university" status in 1964; in 1968, its School of Engineering attained national accreditation, and by 1978, 18 masters programs were offered.

The public school systems of the county operated in three distinct systems: Greensboro City Schools, High Point City Schools, and County Schools. Each had its own administration, policies, and procedures. The three systems were consolidated on July 1, 1993. The system is now governed by an 11-member board of education selected through general elections. The 650-square-mile district has 94 schools. The enrollment makes it the third largest district in North Carolina and one of the top 60 in the United States.

Guilford County continues to be well known for its excellent educational institutions. This has kept the county in a consistent pattern of growth by attracting new industry and new people. The two state universities reflect the positive developments of the 1960s Civil Rights movements: the desegregation of schools allowing all citizens an equal education, the improvement of the African American's role in modern society, and the ascent of women to equal positions in business and commerce.

As all the schools have strengthened their areas of specialization, they have also embraced the community and each other in a cooperation to benefit all students. By the 1970s, the educational systems in Guilford County were an undeniable enterprise involving tens of thousands of students and teachers. Early proponents of education felt that better schools and educational opportunities would be the bridge to the future. Their vision was sound.

Students from the Normal and Industrial School marched down the center of Elm Street on Education Day as part of the Greensboro Centennial. The county boasts a proud tradition of academic excellence. (Courtesy North Carolina Department of Archives and History.)

8. HEALTH AND HEARTH

Adequate health care was an early concern. There were no physicians when David Caldwell arrived in the county to preach in the late eighteenth century. By chance, Dr. Woodsides, a distant cousin of Mrs. Caldwell, came to visit and agreed to stay and practice medicine. He died a year later, and Caldwell began "reading medicine" from Woodsides's medical books. He practiced medicine for 45 years, and for many years was the county's only doctor.

Caldwell had pupils who "read medicine" with him. Dr. Washington Donnell was a "pupil physician" and "did most of the riding," which many early settlers referred to as a "horse-ridin' doctor." Dr. Donnell's biographer stated that he rode more than any other man in North Carolina and was in such demand that he had to hide to take a nap.

Few doctors were willing to risk setting up a practice in the backwoods with no facilities. It was not until after the town of Greensboro was established and a courthouse constructed that doctors moved to the area. By 1826, the medical profession had grown, and pharmacies and doctors advertised widely in local newspapers.

In 1826, Dr. J.A. Foulkes announced his arrival in the August 9 *Patriot*:

> Dr. J.A. Foulkes, having returned from Philadelphia, where he has been attending a course of Medical Lectures in the University of Pennsylvania, respectfully informs his friends and the public in generally, that he intends commencing immediately, the practice of Medicine in its various branches, in the Town of Greensborough, the vicinity, and in the adjoining Counties, when his services are required.
>
> He has purchased the House and Lot owned by Dr. Watson, as well as the whole of his Medicines: These, with the addition of those he purchased in the City of Philadelphia, will make, it is presumed, a Shop not inferior to any in the state. Persons from the country, can be supplied with Medicines on reasonable terms; Physicians whose assortment may be broken, will on application, be supplied at a moderate advance on the prime cost.
>
> Those who require his professional services, may rely on his promptness and punctuality, as well as his best exertions to serve them faithfully—he can promise no more; the tests of his medical skill can only be applied by a candid and generous public, when they become sufficiently acquainted with him.

The pharmacy served a variety of needs for citizens, as this local store illustrates. (Courtesy Farrell Collection, North Carolina Office of Archives and History.)

Dr. D.P. Weir opened the Greensborough Drug and Medicine Store and advertised its opening on July 23, 1839, in the *Patriot*. He advertised long lists of drugs, medicines, and dye stuffs in the local paper, and the store listed 112 items in its stock, including muriate, nitric acid, sulphuric, orris root, blood root, gum arabic, iodine, Iceland moss, Irish moss, cloves, soaps, and soda.

The 1820s and 1830s brought forth numerous so-called remedies from early patent medicine manufacturers. For example, tomato pills—Dr. G.R. Phelps' Compound made entirely of vegetable—were widely advertised in 1839 as a new and valuable remedy for all diseases arising from impurities of the blood and morbid secretions of the liver and stomach. In 1840, Goddard's Orris Tooth-Wash was a popular product at the Greensborough Drug Store. Like most toothpaste today, this product was used for cleaning and preserving the teeth and gums and purifying the breath.

Worms were not an unusual problem for people in the nineteenth century. A new worm medicine received a short article in the *Patriot* on January 7, 1843. It had been advertised through handbills distributed through the area. The paper reported, "A patent Vermifuge is being extensively advertised—the bills being headed with large letters, 'A dead shot for worms.' And no doubt many a 'poor worm of the earth' has found it so."

William Clarkson "Clark" Porter opened a drugstore in 1854. His first store was known as Porter's Drug Store and then Porter and Tate, and remained opened at two different locations until 1951. In 1882, Clark's nephew Will Porter worked as the first registered pharmacist in Guilford County. Will was influenced by friends to move to Texas. As mentioned in previous chapters, he later took the pen name O. Henry, and was known as the famous short-story writer. In 1887, Clark moved his store to Asheboro Street and took George W. Kestler as a partner. The second store remained open until 1951, when the owner, Joseph T. Usher, donated the furnishings to the Greensboro History Museum.

Two ladies hand filled all the Vicks VapoRub jars in 1915. (Courtesy Proctor and Gamble, Greensboro.)

In 1890, Lunsford Richardson Sr. moved to the home of his wife, Mary Lynn Smith, in Greensboro. He purchased the "original" Porter Drug Store in 1891 and was joined by a partner, John Fariss, one of Porter's clerks. They decided on the name "Richardson and Fariss." In those days, the pharmacist prescribed medication and mixed custom doses. Richardson had proven himself as a talented pharmacist and chemist while operating a drugstore in Selma. He set up a small laboratory and analyzed the drugs he compounded. He prepared medications to relieve minor ailments, and he developed 19 products called "Vick's Family Remedies." He decided on the name Vick's as a compliment to his brother-in-law and friend, Dr. Joshua W. Vick. One of the remedies was a vaporizing ointment containing menthol, a new drug for the treatment of respiratory ailments. He developed it as relief for the common cold. The final formulation was a combination of menthol with camphor, oil of eucalyptus, and other ingredients mixed in a special petroleum base. It was introduced in 1894 as "Vick's Magic Croup Salve" and later became known to the world as "Vick's VapoRub."

In 1898, he sold his share in the store and established the L. Richardson Wholesale Drug Company for a greater distribution of the products. The demands of stockholders, suppliers, freight complications, and competition slowed his ability to develop new products, and in 1905, Richardson sold the wholesale business to R.L. Justice and retained his trademarks. He invested his money into the first Pepsi Cola Bottling plant in Greensboro as a method of supporting his family until he could stimulate the sales of Vick products. At the same time, he organized the Vick's Family Remedies Company, which he entirely owned. He continued manufacturing the remedies in two small storerooms located behind the Pepsi plant.

Richardson employed two ladies and one traveling salesman for the Vick's products. Mrs. Hobson and Mrs. Ella Taylor had worked for Mrs. Richardson since 1901 and worked on and off as sales demanded for a salary of $2.50 per week. They weighed out each ingredient for the Vicks Croup and Pneumonia Salve into two 1-gallon kettles and then poured it into jars. Their output was 2 gallons a day. In an interview, Mrs. Taylor recalled that Mr. Richardson gave them free Pepsi drinks while they worked. Richardson would also bring his children in to help when they were not attending school.

In 1907, Richardson's oldest son, H. Smith Richardson, joined the company as the sales manager and put all of his efforts into selling one product—Vicks VapoRub. He had a vision and flair for advertising, and through his efforts, the product was sold throughout the United States.

When the flu epidemic of 1918 struck and lasted until the spring of 1919, millions of patients purchased VapoRub to help relieve their symptoms. Night shifts were added, office workers labored in the plant after supper, salesmen were called off the road to help in the plant, and every dealer was rationed daily. When schools shut down because of the epidemic, schoolteachers worked at Vick's plant filling jars. The night force in 1919 consisted almost 99 percent of returned soldiers from World War I who needed jobs.

It became apparent that Vick's needed machines for mixing and filling in order to increase the daily output of product. A steam-jacketed mixing kettle replaced hand mixing. In 1915, the new piston fillers filled 60 jars a minute.

Up until 1915, Vick's VapoRub was filled one jar at a time by the piston filler pictured in the foreground. The newly installed Karl Kieffer is visible in the background, which filled 60 jars per minute. (Courtesy Proctor and Gamble, Greensboro.)

When Lunsford Richardson Sr. died in 1919, Vick's had become a household word. Smith Richardson became president of the company and was instrumental in Vick's being sold in England and Mexico. The Mexican government's tax made it too expensive for the average Mexican person to afford. The company then devised equipment for mixing and filling so that products could be made and packaged in locations other than the main plant. During the Great Depression, the firm was one of the few places in Greensboro that kept operating.

Doctors and pharmacists came to the county, but there was not a hospital in the first 100 years of the county's history. A group of ten young women formed the West End Club and then affiliated with the King's Daughters and raised $1,543 through organizing entertainment and suppers and asking for donations. It took three years, but they bought a lot on North Greene Street and erected a ten-room hospital for $2,500. They pledged their members for service and convinced three physicians to practice at the facility. On September 3, 1891, the small hospital was opened for both paying and charity patients. Unfortunately, the facility was closed in two years because of the lack of funds.

In 1904, a 12-bed hospital was established in High Point by the Junior Order of American Mechanics, a patriotic fraternity. It was sold to a group of doctors in 1911 and named High Point Hospital. Even though an $18,000 Works Progress Administration grant was offered for hospital improvements, the voters turned down the project mostly because a group of manufacturers objected to incurring municipal debt. The hospital merged with Guilford General in 1944 and became High Point Memorial Hospital.

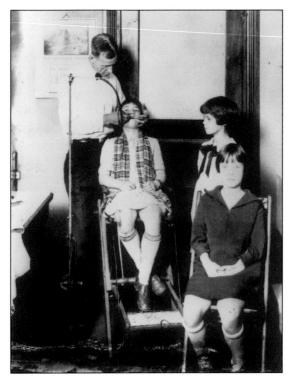

In the 1930s, health professionals regularly visited schools. Dr. Long is shown using portable dentistry equipment as he repairs minor dental problems. (Courtesy Farrell Collection, North Carolina Office of Archives and History.)

116

Left: The Sisters of Charity established the St. Leo's Hospital in Greensboro. The nuns pictured here served as nurses and instructors in the nursing school established by the hospital. Right: Nurses are pictured here after their graduation from the nursing school at St. Leo's Hospital. The school graduated over 600 nurses. (Both images courtesy Farrell Collection, North Carolina Office of Archives and History.)

Ten years passed before another hospital facility was organized in Greensboro. During that time, doctors had to perform major surgeries on kitchen tables, on back porches, or in barns with only the light of a coal oil lamp. Citizens without a residence in Greensboro were often treated in a hotel room. In 1901, six doctors established the Greensboro Hospital with 12 rooms. Dr. J. Wesley Long joined the staff, and the hospital served the local population until St. Leo's Hospital was opened in 1906.

St. Leo's was constructed in Greensboro after Reverend Vincent G. Taylor of St. Benedict's Roman Catholic Church invited the Sisters of Charity to come and establish a hospital. Opened in 1906, it was the first "real" hospital in the city of Greensboro and people came from across the state by horse-drawn conveyances seeking treatment. The Sisters at St. Leo helped everyone, regardless of race, color, or creed. They opened a nursing school, which graduated 600 nurses during the 47 years of operation. The hospital was closed in 1954.

With the opening of a hospital, specialists were attracted to the area. Dr. Perry Reaves established an eye, ear, nose, and throat infirmary. He was the inventor of surgical instruments that were in use throughout the world. In one interesting story, a member of the Winston-Salem Reynolds family traveled to London for a tonsillectomy. He was told by the London specialist that Dr. Reaves of Greensboro was one of the best specialists in his field and that he, the Londoner, was using a Reaves invention to perform the surgery.

117

After the Greensboro Hospital failed, Dr. Wesley Long opened a private 20-bed hospital. He purchased the residence of Branch Merrimon next door to the Pierce Rucker House. The first patient was admitted on May 10, 1917, and because of the war, it was closed on August 4, 1918. Dr. Long also established a medical unit in France and turned his Greensboro facility over to the Red Cross to handle the influenza epidemic. After the war, he built a 23-room surgical annex to his hospital, which opened in 1926. He died the same year. The doctors who purchased the facility changed the name to Wesley Long Hospital.

There was no organized health care for black families until Lunsford Richardson provided visiting nurses in 1914. In 1919, the Trinity Hospital was opened in a private home but proved to be inadequate. Mrs. Lunsford Richardson and Mrs. Emanuel Sternberger made the L. Richardson Hospital possible by personal endowments. The first African-American hospital opened in 1927, and a new hospital opened in 1965. The establishment of a hospital encouraged black physicians to come to Guilford County.

The Moses H. Cone Memorial Hospital was built on North Elm Street in 1953 in memory of textile magnate Moses Cone. His widow, Bertha Lindau Cone, died in 1947 and left a trust to be used to build the facility. Cone Hospital remains the leading facility in the county, and in the 1990s, it merged with Wesley Long to form an extensive health care system.

In the 1880s, Greensboro and High Point commissioners discussed the possibility of establishing water and sewage facilities using public bonds. However, they decided the pure water available was good enough to continue with public wells. When the water supply was inadequate to extinguish the Benbow Hotel fire in 1899 and when there was a drought in 1900, the City of Greensboro decided to take control of the water resources. In July 1915, the water in High Point was described as "being practically as good as boiled water." There were 300 open wells, and typhoid and malaria became part of the history of the county.

During the summer of 1899, there was an increase in contagious diseases in the state. Health authorities warned Guilford County about a possible outbreak of malaria. However, typhoid struck the Normal and Industrial School. The number of cases increased rapidly, and the school was closed. Forty-eight girls were too ill to be taken home and were treated in a dormitory by Dr. Anna Gove, Dr. W.P. Beall, faculty members, and ladies from Greensboro. Many of the students died at the college and some died after returning home. The cause of the epidemic was traced to a defective sewer that had contaminated the main well.

In 1897, High Point appointed five doctors to a board of health. In 1899, an outbreak of smallpox hit High Point. Quarantines and inoculations were legally mandated. A tax of 15¢ per $100 valuation was levied to pay for the public health expense. The health officers required anyone entering the city to provide proof of their immunizations.

In 1913, it was estimated there were 1,500 cases of malaria just in the city of Greensboro, followed by a severe typhoid epidemic in 1915. Flies and mosquitoes created a tremendous problem, and Greensboro began a war on the insects. E.P. Wharton and Dr. Battle acted as "assistant health officers" without pay, and vowed to make Greensboro a "flyless, mosquitoless city." They distributed fly swatters, bought flies for a nickel a dozen,

Milk breaks in elementary schools helped in the fight to eradicate pellagra. (Courtesy Farrell Collection, North Carolina Office of Archives and History.)

passed out flypaper, enlisted Boy Scouts to spray mosquito-breeding areas, fined keepers of unsanitary places, and hired a mosquito expert with experience in Panama. In 1918, High Point employed two sanitary patrolmen to fight flies and mosquitoes. The fight was not effective, because stables and privies outside the city limits produced a ring of flies around both towns. The county residents declared that flies were a part of rural life.

Greensboro gained the reputation of being an unhealthy place, and various organizations, as well as the *Daily News*, tried to combat the unhealthy image by saying, "Greensboro is the very healthiest spot in North Carolina." In 1915, Mrs. W.H. Swift, chairman of the executive council of the PTA, didn't agree. She said, "Babies are in more danger of losing their lives than soldiers at the front. All one could do was stand at their open graves and say, 'Thy will be done.' "[1] Her comments were a result of the smallpox epidemic of 1915 and 1916.

The Spanish Influenza arrived in September 1918 during World War I. So many cases were reported that all public places, including schools and churches, were closed throughout the county. High Point Mayor William Preston Ragan died, as did the entire family of Ed Bryant, a veteran of World War I. The newspapers in the county reported on the efforts of orphaned children trying to hold their families together.

Interwoven with this period was the plight of the poor. In the 1930s, the High Point Red Cross launched a campaign to eradicate pellagra, a disease that affected many of the poor due to their deficient diets. By 1937, 200 families were receiving free dairy products everyday.

There was no public health service, and help was distributed at the discretion of the various mayors throughout the county. Organizations were formed to give aid, but the population grew so quickly that in 1917, the county commission received strong appeals from the citizens and made plans to create a department of social services. The commissioners initially tried to reject the appeals because they claimed the county's

Red Cross workers are shown here at the Greensboro Train Station during World War I. (Courtesy Greensboro Historical Museum.)

debt was "so heavy and needs so great." Mrs. W.H. Swift, the PTA leader, pointed out that although the county was too poor to have a social welfare program and too poor to protect its children, it was able "to build a $500,000 courthouse to try them in when they go astray."[2] The commissioners yielded, and by 1919, Guilford County was one of two counties to hire a superintendent of public welfare. The commissioners created a furor when they funded welfare and discontinued the public library appropriation. Then, welfare began extending to prisoners. The jail had been compared to the "Black Hole of Calcutta" since the late 1800s. A new county jail was constructed in 1902 and the Board of Public Welfare called for the firing of inhumane guards.

Poliomyelitis hit Guilford County in 1947, and by 1948, every available space was full of patients. Temporary facilities were created in a building at the old World War II Overseas Replacement Depot and at the former offices of the North Carolina Employment Service. Greensboro became the medical center for 16 counties, and hospital facilities were urgently needed.

Newspapers and radio stations asked the public for help. Within 14 days, more than $100,000 was donated. Plans were drawn for the 125-bed Central Carolina Convalescent Hospital. Union men worked side by side with non-union men, and 11,000 hours were donated by volunteer workmen. Within 94 days, the hospital opened to care for the polio patients.

While the county passed from one century to another, it changed from an agrarian economy to an industrial economy. This brought about changes from a pedestrian society to a mobile population. Churches made the greatest contributions to family life and social interaction. The county benefited from the religious foundation that was laid from the first settlements in the county.

Before the Civil War, there were annual camp meeting revivals, called protracted meetings, attended by black and white people of all denominations. At one session, there were 23 ministers representing 6 different faiths. These meetings were so well attended that the individual denominations started their own revivals. In 1833, the Presbyterian churches established an all-Presbyterian meeting ground. At the turn of the twentieth century, protracted meetings were popular. Multitudes of people attended sermons and speeches. At the time, churches moved beyond the city center and many denominations established missionary churches in new neighborhoods. In High Point and Gibsonville, storeowners benefited from sales during the these special times.

From 1910 to 1926, Chautauqua was the cultural event of the summer. It began as an educational festival in western New York and expanded into a touring show. The Chautauqua that came to Guilford County was a production of the Redpath organization and was a series of performances by talented entertainers. It was endorsed as educational and cultural by the chambers of commerce, churches, politicians, and ladies' societies. A special feature was Billy Sunday, an ex–baseball player turned preacher. Just to see him wrestle with the "Invisible Devil" was worth the price of admission. As soon as the Chautauqua tents were struck, another revival tent went up immediately and an evangelist would stay for as many nights as he could draw a crowd.

The original churches in the county prospered and gave rise to many other churches. As the suburbs developed, the church members took on a missionary zeal to organize new neighborhood churches. First Presbyterian Church was organized in 1825 by Reverend William Paisley when he began services in his Male Academy. It grew to become the largest church in Greensboro and helped to establish many churches, including Asheboro Street Presbyterian Church, the New Bessemer Avenue Church, the North Elm Church, and the Walker Avenue Church, which served the Normal and Industrial School neighborhood.

The first sanctuary for the Presbyterian Church of the Covenant was built in 1916 near the the Normal and Industrial School campus. (Courtesy Presbyterian Church of the Covenant.)

A neighborhood of fine homes had grown up adjacent to the new Normal and Industrial School to house the growing needs of professors, administrators, and families. The pastor of the First Presbyterian Church was walking with a group near the college and spoke of the need for a Presbyterian presence to serve the college and the neighborhood. In May 1906, a group of 69 people petitioned the Orange Presbytery requesting the construction of the Walker Avenue Presbyterian Church. The structure was completed later that year at a cost of $4,800, and Reverend R. Murphy Williams became the first minister. In 1909, the name of the church was changed to Presbyterian Church of the Covenant. The original wooden sanctuary was contributed for the establishment of the Glenwood Presbyterian Church in 1914 and a modern brick church was designed by architect Harry Barton and built on the site.

The Methodists came to the county in 1770 when Andrew Yeargan was appointed to the Yadkin Circuit. After the Guilford Circuit was established, the Methodists claimed 551 white and 39 black members. Some Methodists attended First Presbyterian services when a minister was not available. The church constructed a sanctuary in 1831 and officially began as Greensboro Methodist Episcopal Church. When the congregation constructed their third sanctuary on West Market Street, the name changed to West Market Street Methodist. The congregation began the Greensboro Female College in 1832, only one year after their first sanctuary was completed. Through their outreach, seven other churches were organized, including the Proximity Methodist Church and the College Place Methodist Church.

West Market Street Methodist Church is the oldest Methodist congregation in Greensboro. Their third church, seen here c. 1925, was constructed in 1893 and is still in use today. (Courtesy Farrell Collection, North Carolina Office of Archives and History.)

Growth and development in Guilford County pushed agricultural interest into the rural areas, and modern roads were needed to connect those areas with the markets of Greensboro, High Point, and Jamestown. (Courtesy Farrell Collection, North Carolina Office of Archives and History.)

The first Jewish settlers in High Point and Greensboro arrived about 1895. The Jewish faithful came together to worship in the early 1900s. Records of the Greensboro Hebrew congregation began in 1909. All people of Jewish faith worked together for the construction of a temple, and Temple Emanuel was built and dedicated in 1923. In 1945, the group divided into two congregations—Orthodox and Conservative.

Our Lady of Grace Catholic Church was established and built as a tribute to Julian Price's wife, Ethel Clay Price, after her death in 1943. Mr. Price completed arrangements for the church building with Bishop Vincent Waters and donated $400,000. Mr. Price died in 1946, before the building could be completed. Rising building costs caused the construction to be postponed. Price's children donated an additional $300,000 to complete the memorial to their mother, and the first Mass was celebrated on Sunday, September 14, 1952.

Therefore, Guilford passed from a county of villages and small towns to a transportation center that attracted new citizens of vision who came seeking opportunities. Rapid population growth led to a need for housing and services. The enhancements of neighborhoods, schools, churches, and hospitals put the county on a success track that assured a bright future. The good came with the bad, as the citizens worked through the demands of modernization. Growing cities and towns needed good roads, business diversity, and local government.

9. Entering the Modern Era

In 1890, there was an urgent cry for road improvements that were already well over 30 years past due and were as much a topic of conversation as the weather. Several generations had grown to adulthood and no action had been taken. Dirt roads turned to mud during rains and were often left deeply rutted. The rain brought deep mud holes. There was no system of roads; therefore, the roads throughout the county impeded every outing, from a trip to church on Sunday to the transportation of goods to market.

In 1891, T. Gilbert Pearson left the Guilford College train station. He made his way up the road to the college through "one continuous sticky mass of the reddest mud" he had ever seen. It was slick and he stated that "several times my feet utterly deserted me." Another resident reported that the state of the country roads was a quicksand bed where "the mule went out of sight."[1] By 1892, the editor of the *Patriot* was asking, "Are we destined for all time to founder?" In March 1892, citizens faced with a municipal election were instructed through editorials in the the *Patriot* to remember that the commissioners "had the sole power of levying taxes and properly expending the same."

A citizen who was referred to as a "pubic spirited man" suggested paving the streets with stone. He offered to cover the entire expense of working two hands constantly on the streets using mules to pull the wagon and tools for the total amount of $1,000.

It was not until 1899, the year Guilford County passed a Road Law, that serious work was completed on the roads. A tax was levied for the purpose of road maintenance. However, even after the taxes were collected, the road supervisor's life was in danger if he attempted even the smallest realignment of the road.

Males between the ages of 18 and 45, who worked without pay six days a year, maintained the roads. The responsibilities of road building and repair were enforced by laws much like those in the 1700s. Methods of completing construction projects were impractical; the men furnished their own tools, and there was no budget.

In 1900, David Schenck recorded in his diary that the road to the battleground was impassable. Even in good weather, it took him as much as four hours to travel the 16.32 miles from Jefferson Square in Greensboro to Washington and Main Streets in High Point.

Mecklenburg County had led the way in road construction in 1879 by levying a road tax and building a system of macadam roads, which became an example for other counties.

The entrance to the North Carolina Normal and Industrial School on College Avenue was newly paved and landscaped in this c. 1928 view. Until the mid-1920s, the avenue was known for being paved in mud when it rained, and in dust in dry weather.

In 1899, J. Van Lindley led the way for Guilford County to finally construct decent thoroughfares. He is credited with spearheading the formation of the Good Roads Club.

Road legislation in 1901 resulted in one-third of the counties adopting the Mecklenburg Plan. Around 1902, a "good roads train" crossed North Carolina. Demonstrations of road building were given and "good roads" conventions were held. On February 12 and 13, 1902, the North Carolina Good Roads Association was formally organized, which gave impetus to highway development throughout North Carolina and ultimately resulted in the establishment of a State Highway Commission. By 1903, the local group received a $300,000 bond and established the Guilford Highway Commission.

By 1910, 99 miles of hard surface roads had been constructed throughout Guilford County. The macadam roads were created when crushed granite, earth, and water were mixed. It was immediately successful, especially for horse-drawn vehicles. When cars began regularly using the roads, the gravel was scattered or the weight of the vehicle caused it to sink into the ground, creating unevenness of the road surface. Highway 10 through Gibsonville was one of the first macadamized roads in the state.

The MacAdam process was invented by John MacAdam, who was the developer of the first road-paving material. In 1770, he emigrated from Scotland to New York to work. He returned to Scotland in 1783 and experimented with road construction. He developed the "modern" process when he became the surveyor of the Bristol Turnpike in 1816. He further developed the process of creating a slightly convex road surface to ensure that rainwater would drain off and not penetrate the foundation. MacAdam died in 1836, but by the end of the nineteenth century, most of the main roads in Europe and the United States used his process. The name "macadam" became widely known, and into the 1960s, roads were sometimes referred to as the "macadam."

After years of traveling throughout the county with a horse-drawn cart, Lewis Harris saved enough money to open a store on Main Street in High Point c. 1915. (Courtesy Harris family private collection.)

In 1889, the Greensboro police department became an official agency, and the first police force reported on July 11. The duties of the five-man force included tax collecting until May 1892, when Chief of Police R.M. Reese resigned his duties and became the first full-time tax collector. Telephones came into use in 1894 and revolutionized the police department. The City returned R.M. Reese to his old job as chief of police and the officers once again collected taxes.

An early High Point businessman, Lewis Harris was a teenage peddler from Russian who arrived in High Point in 1898 with a pack on his back. He had come seeking new customers for his products and soon became one of the first merchants in the area. From High Point, he traveled the wagon roads from house to house and village to village on foot with the pack on his back because he could not afford a horse.

In 1938, Lewis Harris was interviewed by Staley A. Cook of the *High Point Enterprise*. Harris recalled that he once traveled with Herbert Johnson, "That was in the backpack days when Cleveland was president. I carried the pack and it was pretty heavy on the start. Mr. Johnson would say to me, 'Lewis, why do you carry such a heavy pack?' I'd reply, I'm expecting it to be dollars lighter when I get along the route."

Dr. Donald Harris recalled the stories he had heard as a child from his Grandfather Lewis Harris:

> He [Lewis Harris] arrived in the year when there was a financial panic. He was
> out searching for a place of opportunity. As he improved his financial status,
> he traveled by horse and wagon. If he was going to be gone for a few days or

overnight, he used to talk about the good Quaker families who would invite him for a meal and to sleep in their barns. Sometimes he would be invited in to sleep if they had enough room. But back then, families had a lot of children and places to sleep were hard to find.

Harris's daughter-in-law, Jean Harris, remembered how industrious, generous, and public-spirited her father-in-law was. She stated, "He was one of the first Jewish people in High Point; however he liked all people—Jew and Gentile."

Staley Cook pointed out that Harris was a pioneer and a successful merchant. Harris described the old wagon trails of the time as follows: "They were rugged and settlers were squatted here and there. Miles separated them and in between were virgin forests of pine and oak." When Harris arrived in the farmyard, he was welcomed from the time the family heard him call "Whoa!" to his horse Charlie. Harris visited many Guilford County families including the Hoovers, the Walkers, the Currins, the Mendenhalls, and other old homesteaders. The worst experience he had was when his old horse Charlie got mired in a ditch, still hitched to a fully loaded wagon. People from all around came to help in the rescue.

In the *Enterprise* article, Harris said, "It was not a time encouraging for a man to enter business, or should it be said, the average man. But for a man who would take the bottom rung facing the hot sun of summer upon the footpath, the chill blast of ice and snow of winter—for a man who was frugal, who had saved, the next rung was an easy climb." Lewis quit the trails to open a store on Main Street in High Point, then a mere village of a few hundred people, a factory or two, a couple of stores, and two churches. Main Street was dusty and muddy according to the weather. The "whiteway" flickered with flames from the oil lamps, which William Rumley cleaned and filled, as a sideline from his duty as sexton of one of the churches.

There was a well located in front of Harris's store on Main Street. Harris remembered the following regarding the well and its social function:

> I used to take care of that well and supplied it with a dipper. A pump brought the water up, refreshing to man and beast who came from the backwoods hills of Guilford into town to trade. A trough was handy for the horses and hitching posts lined the street. Most men had to have his "chaw" and his wife might have her "dip" but the men could hit a sawdust filled box fifteen feet away. The ladies were more secretive.

Lewis Harris was a member of the original bucket brigade for High Point's fire department. He and his wife, Ida, married in 1901, raised five children. Along with many other items, he sold men's clothing in his store. A good suit only cost from $4.50 to $9. Harris's brother was a partner for 35 years, and when Lewis's son Jake was older, he entered the business. Lewis Harris became a wealthy and beloved figure in early High Point. He also helped establish the Jewish faith there.

Jake Harris followed in his father's footsteps by learning the retail business. After several years, he established his own business, which became a fixture in High Point.

Jake's wife, Jean, remembers the first years when they sold used furniture and delivered it for free: "We couldn't afford a truck, so we moved unbelievable things in our car. I was so happy when we had saved the money to buy a second-hand truck."

Jake Harris, too, witnessed many milestones in High Point's growth. Born in 1903, he was in the first town's Boy Scout troop, which was organized in 1914. He was active in the National Guard and was a life member of the Scottish Rite Temple and the Oasis Temple for 75 years. He organized the clown club and was a member of the Governor's Committee for the handicapped. On June 15, 1965, he received a Presidential Citation from President Lyndon Johnson for his community service. He was the first person to speak to the Jaycees for brotherhood in the United States. He married Jean Ershler, a rabbi's daughter, on September 3, 1931, and lived to be 96 years of age.

In the 1890s, a horse-drawn streetcar that ran on a single track was brought to Greensboro. Actually, an old mule did the pulling. When the beast couldn't make the grade, passengers got off and helped push the vehicle. In 1902, the Greensboro Electric Company inaugurated electric streetcars. They ran from East Market Street out West Market and Spring Garden Streets to Lindley Park and as far north as Proximity and White Oak Mills. J. Van Lindley provided land at Lindley Park, the west end of the trolley line, and an amusement park with a pavilion, artificial lake, casino, and bowling alleys were constructed. The amusement park was closed in 1917. The streetcars were operated by a succession of companies until Duke Power took them over and operated them into the 1950s.

In the 1880s, a sewage system became necessary for the populated areas and the need for vitrified salt-glazed sewer pipe arose. J. Van Lindley ran a nursery in the Pomona area just

The Perley Thomas Car Works began building streetcars in High Point in the late 1800s. It later became known as Thomas Built Buses. (Courtesy High Point Historical Museum.)

By 1912, High Point took on the look of a city. Beautiful residences built along South Main also had streetcar service. (Courtesy North Carolina Office of Archives and History.)

outside of Greensboro. Lindley and his assistant, Charles Boren, were aware that women in the neighborhood used a special clay from the farm of A.Y. Smith to whitewash their fireplaces. They also knew that Smith made small tiles and firebrick and they felt the same clay might manufacture drain pipe. On August 12, 1886, a group met in the back room of the Porter and Dalton Drug Store and organized the Pomona Terra Cotta Company. They formed a partnership of Lindley, Boren, and Dr. John E. Logan and bought the Smith farm and organized the Pomona Terra Cotta Company in 1886. They also involved William Boren's brothers Gurney, Charles, Richard, and Cecil. They paid their workers $1 a day, and using a 2-horsepower engine, a boiler, and two wood-burning kilns, they created agricultural drain tiles. It took them nearly 15 years of experimentation to produce a standard approved sewer pipe.

They expanded to other products after they gained success by selling sewer pipe to other cities and towns. The company grew to four plants by 1923, and by 1955, their brand of sewer pipe was widely used. Among their other products were conduit tile, flue linings, firebricks, tiles, and chimney tops.

While Lewis Harris was establishing his career as a merchant, the Cone brothers were ending their careers as salesmen. Moses Cone and his brother, Ceasar, were working in their father's wholesale grocery business when they thought that textile manufacturing might be a good business for them to engage. They traveled for their father's wholesale grocery business in Baltimore and called on general stores in small towns all over the South. Many of the stores were "company stores" for employees of textile mills. The brothers realized the need for textile development, and they invested with a partner in a mill. They teamed with C.E. Graham and opened a manufacturing company in Asheville in 1887.

The Cone brothers built the Proximity Manufacturing Company in 1895. They selected the name because of the plant's "proximity" to the cotton fields and gins. The name was changed to Cone Mills Corporation in 1948. The plant is seen here c. 1899. (Courtesy North Carolina Office of Archives and History.)

With 50 mills throughout the South, Moses Cone had a vision of promoting the sale of cloth. He convinced other mill owners to allow him to market their goods through the Cone Export and Commission Company. The Cones incorporated the company in 1890 and established headquarters in New York City. The brothers then moved to Greensboro to build their mills, mainly because the city had railroad service radiating in six directions.

Because of their knowledge of the textile business, coupled with their vision of the future, the Cones also established other textile-related businesses, including the Southern Finishing and Warehouse Company. They took over C.E. Graham's manufacturing, their original mill, and renamed it the Asheville Cotton Mill. J.A. Odell, a successful Greensboro businessman, is said to have remarked, "Grab hold of their coattails, boys, and don't let them get away."[2]

The Cones brothers purchased over 2,000 acres of land in northeast Greensboro and built the Proximity Cotton Mill to operate as a denim mill. They were joined by their younger brothers Solomon, Julius, Bernard, Clarence, and Fred. The Cones convinced their friends Emanuel and Herman Sternberger to move to Greensboro and build a flannel factory in 1898. It was a revolutionary new fabric, and the Sternbergers named the mill the "Revolution." The Cones built the White Oak Cotton Mill, and it became the largest denim mill in the world. Cone Mills Corporation also produced corduroys, twills, suedes, towels, and wash cloths.

In 1899, Wysong and Miles began manufacturing machinery for other industries. They began as a small operation and manufactured products by special orders. The company produced machinery for making furniture, automobiles, airplanes, television cabinets, and refrigerators. During World War II, orders for woodworking machinery decreased, and Wysong developed procedures and manufacturing for the metal-working industry and became one of the South's first machine tool builders. In the 1950s, they produced woodworking machinery that was used in furniture plants.

On July 2, 1912, the board of the Jefferson Standard Life Insurance Company voted to move its home office from Raleigh to Greensboro. When Security Life and Jefferson Standard merged, the majority of directors were from Greensboro. By 1916, they had formulated plans to build a skyscraper. The 17-story headquarters was completed in October 1923 and was the tallest building between Baltimore and Houston—and it was considered the tallest building in the South. Julian Price rose from a job as a railway telegrapher and eventually became president of the prestigious company. Price is credited with getting Jefferson Standard Life through the Great Depression.

By 1921, there was a total of five life insurance and four fire insurance companies headquartered in Greensboro. In 1924, Southern Life and Trust changed its name to Pilot Life Insurance Company. Another insurance business, Dixie Life Insurance Company moved to Newark, New Jersey.

By 1914, Guilford County was enjoying a great period of growth and prosperity. The progress of the war in Europe was closely followed by the citizens, and they were relieved when Woodrow Wilson broadcast that "it was not America's fight." However, on April 6, 1917, the United States was drawn into the war, and 1,621 men and 13 nurses from Greensboro went off to fight the "war to end all wars."

In High Point, 1,700 young men registered for the draft, and within the first few months, 97 were selected for service. At home, older men doubled their work to relieve the younger men for service, and citizens were purchasing war bonds. Industries throughout the county converted production from furniture to airplane propellers and wagon parts, and textile makers produced apparel for the "effort." Freight marked for the war effort received first priority; anything for domestic use was always delayed. The first list of casualties reached the area in June 1918.

Jefferson Standard Life Insurance moved their headquarters from Raleigh to Greensboro and constructed a 17-story office building on land where the Guilford County Courthouse stood. The new site became known as Jefferson Square.

Women came together to make clothing, to knit, and to roll bandages. Manufacturing plants adjusted their schedules to fill war needs. Families grew gardens and preserved vegetables for the war effort. Students from the Normal School volunteered to work on the college farm during one summer and were able to raise and can 8,000 gallons of vegetables. Just as the war effort was taking a toll on the citizens, the Spanish Flu arrived in Guilford County in September 1918. By mid-October, there were over 1,000 cases, and over 50 people died, including the mayor of High Point, W.P. Ragan. Throughout the county, all public assemblies were banned, including schools and churches.

In November 1918, World War I ended, and the *High Point Enterprise* ran the headline, "Germany Capitulates." A number of soldiers, however, were not filled with great joy when they returned, for they discovered that members of their family had died from the flu while they were gone. Private Edward Bryant had been in one of the first groups of soldiers to leave High Point. He served throughout the entire war, was severely wounded, and returned home in January 1919 to find that his mother, father, and one of his sisters had died from the flu epidemic.

Following World War I, the piedmont experienced another period of rapid industrial expansion and population growth. The Carolina Steel and Iron Company was organized to produce structural steel, which was used to construct schools, churches, and factories. It was stronger, more durable, and more economical than other materials and could also be used in construction of highway bridges. Thirteen Guilford County stockholders founded the company, including William C. Boren, W.B. Truitt, and J.W. McLennan.

During the 1920s, High Point's economy increased and the city realized enormous prosperity. Twenty-six textile plants were in operation in addition to furniture manufacturing. The town proclaimed itself, "the Hosiery Capital of the South." Two

Company M, High Point Rifles, is shown here ready to leave for duty in World War I. (Courtesy High Point Historical Museum.)

Seen here c. 1930, the Hotel Sheraton was High Point's first hotel with modern construction.

ten-story structures were constructed in 1921—the Sheraton Hotel and the Commercial National Bank. Roads were paved, public parks were developed, and new schools were constructed to meet the needs of the growing population. When the city limits expanded, another 6,500 people were added to the city tax rolls. Political dissension developed between High Point and Greensboro. High Point was surpassing the "other place" in size, development, industry, and population, and the citizens and leaders were displeased when county commissioners spent High Pointers' money for improvement that benefited Greensboro. Secession was proposed. In 1913, Thomas J. Gold, a state legislator, introduced the "Aycock County Bill," which called for the creation of a new county by taking portions of Guilford, Randolph, and Davidson County with High Point as the county seat. The general assembly rejected the bill. By 1923, High Point was the sixth largest city in the state, surpassing Greensboro by 3,000 people. During this decade, High Point surpassed Greensboro and became a model industrial city.

There was population growth throughout the county. Commissioners and city planners had to face the fact that the development of industry would bring growth in population. There was a focus on neighborhoods, and certain areas were developed that were exclusive, leaving out the working-class families. In High Point, Emerywood was developed, and in Greensboro, Irving Park grew, as prosperous industrialists and merchants moved from the inner city. This new prosperity and mobility set the stage for urbanization.

In 1927, politicians, businessmen, and citizens were realizing the decades-old dream of the increased status of Guilford County in the state. This elevation of importance over other counties was due to it becoming a central transportation center and developer of new industry. The new Southern Railway passenger terminal opened in the county. In

May 1927, the Greensboro–High Point airport opened in the area once known as the Friendship community, and a two-lane, paved road was opened connecting High Point and Greensboro.

During the 1890s, several railroad lines declared bankruptcy. J.P. Morgan, one of the country's richest bankers, organized the Southern Railway Company and in 1894 purchased or leased the lines that routed through Guilford County. With only one railroad company in control, it eradicated all competitors and higher freight rates ensued. Development was crippled because profits from shipped goods were reduced and new businesses were discouraged from locating in the county. When the company realized reduction of business, they improved services by expanding facilities and advertising for new customers. In 1904, the Southern Railway Division Freight Office moved from Raleigh to Greensboro, and by 1905, two ticket offices were open just in Greensboro. High Point built a new brick passenger station in 1907, and a brick station was built in Gibsonville. In the early 1900s, McLeansville was a developing community and citizens demanded a new passenger station. Because there was a great deal of freight activity at the Pomona yards outside of Greensboro, the Southern Railway expanded the storage space to hold 21 locomotives and built a new coal chute that held 1,000 tons. The new roundhouse had an electrically operated turntable. One of the most luxurious trains in the world, the "Palm Limited," was scheduled to travel from Jacksonville to New York and stopped in Greensboro.

With such important additions to the county's service, the citizens of Greensboro felt the need for a new passenger station. The Greensboro station was out of date, inadequate, dilapidated, and an embarrassment, and according to some, city officials had "no class." In 1923, Greensboro expanded its city limits to 17.84 square miles and began calling itself "Greater Greensboro." The citizens felt that a station befitting "a city" was urgently needed and a furor arose concerning a new facility. Southern Railway declined to finance

The new Southern Railway Station is shown here under construction. Today, the depot is being transformed into a transportation center. (Courtesy Farrell Collection, North Carolina Office of Archives and History.)

a new depot so other plans were developed; in 1923, the voters approved a bond for over a million dollars for the construction of a new depot. Southern Railway decided it was better to control their own property and built the new station without local funding.

In 1927, thousands of people jammed Davie and Washington Streets for the grand opening of the station. There were bands and speeches, and it was one of the largest celebrations the city had ever known. For years, the train was the easiest and quickest way for citizens in Gibsonville, Whitsett, High Point, Jamestown, Summerfield, and Greensboro to do business. With the new station, people flocked into Greensboro to shop for the day and then return home. Throughout the 1930s, Greensboro merchants advertised for patrons to come by train to spend the day shopping in the city.

When Congress authorized the postmaster general to contract with private parties for carrying airmail, the idea of a flying service intrigued county businessmen and politicians. The federal government surveyed routes to the south from Washington, and the triad formed by High Point, Winston-Salem, and Greensboro was a natural stopping point because it was halfway to a number of destinations.

Local historian Ethel Arnett recorded a story about how the chamber of commerce assisted in establishing the airport. In the office of the Greensboro Chamber of Commerce, a yardstick was placed on a map showing a direct line from New York to New Orleans. Letters were sent to every chamber of commerce on that line requesting cooperation with developing a Southern air route. Members did a great deal of work before a petition was signed in 1927 by all the postmasters on the line from New York to New Orleans by way of Greensboro and Atlanta. The Greensboro group continued working in cooperation with High Point and Winston-Salem and requested that the federal government establish a Southern line. Pitcairn Aviation, Incorporated was given the contract to fly a route from New York to Atlanta, with Greensboro as one of five stops. This was the second official air route organized in the United States.

Greensboro, High Point, and Winston-Salem joined together and made plans for an airport. Seven sites were proposed within Guilford County; however, Winston-Salem proposed a site near Kernersville in Forsyth County. Greensboro ultimately chose a site toward Winston-Salem, yet still in Guilford County. They maneuvered to get a field and had the use of the land owned by Paul C. Lindley before they actually made the official purchase of the property. The County purchased 112.7 acres of land from Lindley for $21,250. Greensboro furnished $16,500 and High Point paid $5,000.

The field was cleared by teams of mules. Trees were felled and low places were filled to make the ground as level as possible. A ceremony, with over 12,000 in attendance, was held in May 1927, even though there were no facilities—not even a paved runway. In addition to the large crowd, there were observation planes, bombers from military bases, and officials from Pitcairn Aviation. The airport was named Lindley Field, after Paul C. Lindley, the original owner of the land. The airstrip was also referred to as the Tri-City Airport. In the fall of 1927, Charles A. Lindbergh paid a much-acclaimed visit to Greensboro. He landed at the airport, attended a luncheon in his honor, and made a personal appearance at the Memorial Stadium.

Greensboro leased the airport property from the county for $1 a year and joined with the county to finance improvements. Pitcairn Aviation built a hangar, Greensboro built

This is the first passenger plane before it left Greensboro on November 6, 1930. (Courtesy Farrell Collection, North Carolina Office of Archives and History.)

a terminal, the U.S. government established a weather bureau, and the Department of Commerce set up a radio beam station. In 1928, a schedule for regular airmail service was announced. On May 1, 1928, a huge crowd gathered at the Tri-City Airport to witness North Carolina's first batch of mail "go by air." Over 23,000 pieces of mail were to fly by a special plane to Richmond, Virginia. Greensboro's Mayor Jeffress and Postmaster R.C. Chandley were on hand to greet the pilot, Syd Molloy, and wish him well. Mailbags were then loaded, and young ladies cut ribbons, symbolically beginning the first scheduled airmail service of North Carolina.

On November 6, 1930, passenger service was begun by the Dixie Flying Service, with the first flight from Greensboro to Washington, D.C. Within a year, all services were assumed by Pitcairn Aviation under its new name—Eastern Air Transport Service. They flew 18 passenger Condor planes.

With the full impact of the Great Depression, services dwindled and schedules were cut. There were no paved runways, and the only times that planes could easily take-off or land were during dry weather. The Federal Aviation Administration (FAA) closed the airport. The Civil Works Administration and the Works Progress Administration came to the rescue. The airport was reopened on May 17, 1937, as the Greensboro–High Point Airport. In July 1942, the Greensboro–High Point Airport Authority was created to give the responsibilities of the airport to one single group. In the same year, World War II interrupted the plans for the airport, as the Army Air Corps took over the facilities solely for military use and citizens had no passenger air service and no airmail.

By 1929, Guilford County had attracted a diversified number of manufacturing concerns. But no amount of success could stop the Great Depression. The closing of the banks in 1929 was felt; however, it was in 1931 that unemployment was seriously rising, causing tax payments to fall. City employees, including policemen, were laid off.

People with jobs worked on highly reduced work schedules, and mill workers' hours were severely cut when orders for goods fell off. High Point and Greensboro created emergency programs, and the unemployed were given minor construction jobs on city and county properties. The AME Zion Church helped to care for many unemployed black citizens. A service agency sponsored garden plots so that families could learn to raise some of their own food. There was a huge reduction in the market for all products. The furniture factories and textile mills struggled but were able to stay in business. In 1933, the federal government provided funds for works projects throughout the country, and in High Point alone, 12 projects were completed.

When federal relief came, it was a welcome boost to the economy of the county as well as for morale. It gave High Point a new water and sewage station, street grading, construction of a gymnasium at High Point College, a new post office on Main Street, and improvements to the city lake park, which had previously been constructed on the Deep River with city funding. A new park was built on the city reservoir and included one of the largest swimming pools in the South, which is still a major recreational destination for families today. Considered "a monument to the depression," Greensboro's Country Park was also created as a federal project. The park opened on July 4, 1934, with a lake, a zoo, and a picnic area.

The most noteworthy federal project in the county was the lowering of the railroad tracks routed through High Point. The tracks were the site of constant traffic jams and also of numerous fatalities. Construction began on July 3, 1937, and the first train passed through on March 29, 1938. The first phase of the project was completed in September 1939, but the depot renovations, additional bridge supports, and bridge reinforcements were not completed until 1947.

The building of High Point's post office, seen here c. 1935, was a Federal Works Project.

The Cone's White Oak Mill was built in 1905 and was the biggest denim mill in the world. It was named for the 200-year-old white oak tree that stood on the heavily wooded property where the mill was constructed.

One of the more unusual projects was a meat cannery that opened on Commerce Place in Greensboro in 1934. One hundred seventy workers canned over a million and a half cans of beef, which all went for the relief of the poor and needy. The project was developed when cows were removed from the Dust Bowl in the West for fattening in the piedmont. Over 70,000 cattle were ultimately processed at the cannery.

In the late 1930s, the economic climate began improving across Guilford County, as manufacturers and merchants saw an increase in demand. At that time, High Point began pulling out of the economic depression; in 1936, the Southern Furniture Exposition, celebrating its 15th anniversary, enjoyed record sales. On July 7, 1938, Cone Mills added another day to its work schedule due to the improved demand for goods. Herman Cone, president of Proximity Mill, announced that orders had increased and that the workers were on a schedule of 24 hours per employee, which added 8 hours of work for each.

As the Depression came to an end, life returned to normal. Little did anyone know that the county would only enjoy three years of relative complacency before the horrendous news of December 7, 1941, would bring shortages, relocation, and national upheaval as the United States entered World War II.

10. BIG CHANGES IN GROWTH AND INDUSTRY

When the United States entered World War II, all Guilfordians "went to war." Local men were immediately called up for the draft; thousands volunteered for service; citizens at home grew "victory gardens," conserved everything, participated in rationing, and purchased savings bonds; and local women who had never worked before took jobs in the mills and machine shops, replacing the absent men.

Cone Mills and other mills, including Proximity Mill and Blue Bell, made fabric for the war effort; even if the companies had to retool, these mills manufactured weaves that were needed for tents, sandbags, camouflage, and uniforms. The Vick plant ran 24 hours a day, 7 days a week, and produced drugs and medicines that were sent to the front for the treatment of soldiers. One of Vick's divisions made some of the original uranium salts used in making the atom bomb. The manufacturing division continued to stock drugstores for domestic use. Ammonium perchlorate was made to meet the needs of the army, and this ammonium perchlorate plant was financed, built, and operated by Vick at a substantial loss. One of the Vick family of companies retooled to make machined brass fittings for combat ships.

During World War II, Carolina Steel produced bows for landing craft, deck structures for ships, gun mounts, and portable barges. The company also fabricated steel for war plants and government agency buildings. Carolina Steel received the Army-Navy "E" Award for excellence.

Even though many of the manufacturers in Guilford County received war contracts, many dropped into a slump. When the army was searching for a training facility site, Greensboro promoted itself as a fitting location. The Army Air Force Basic Training Center No. 10 opened on 600 acres in northeast Greensboro and became the only camp in America located entirely in a municipality. On March 1, 1943, thousands of soldiers arrived by train to become the first of 330,000 servicemen to be processed. The center operated for four years as the largest military installation in the United States. It was built on 652 acres east of Summit Avenue at a cost of $8.5 million. Nine hundred forty-four structures were built, including a 1,000-bed hospital, 9 post exchanges, 5 chapels, and 3 movie theaters.

The camp gave the area's economy a boost and became the life-blood of the entire county. It provided over a thousand civilian jobs, and the amount of money spent by military personnel at the local businesses totaled into the millions of dollars. The greatest use of the train facilities in Greensboro came during this time. Thousands of Army Air Force personnel arrived and departed, as the training center was the principal eastern departure point for Air Force personnel going to Europe. The war years were the height of train travel with 38 passenger trains a day serving Greensboro. A USO was organized on North Elm Street, and many churches sponsored special programs to entertain the young military men. Many citizens of the county opened their homes.

In 1942, the Women's College celebrated its 50th anniversary with the opening of the Weatherspoon Art Gallery, named for Elizabeth M. Weatherspoon. Area colleges did their share for the war effort. The ROTC program at A&T College was a source for young, talented black officers. Late in 1942, military training facilities were filled, so the armed forces decided to allow college-bound men to enroll in college rather than wait to be called-up. These men were called into reserve units but did not have a specific date to report for duty. Some of these men attended Guilford College. Once they arrived, they formed a drill platoon on their own. The 1943 *Quaker* raised questions about "military men marching on Guilford's campus." In March 1943, the members of the group were called to active duty, and the number of men on campus dropped from 157 to 61.

On September 24, 1943, a mock invasion of the city of Greensboro was staged as a training exercise. The *Greensboro Daily News* reported the following:

> Soldiers in full battle dress, their faces streaked with dirt, their guns chattering, progressed toward the smoke-filled center of the city. They crouched behind cars, telephone poles and bushes. The scene was given a Pied Piper tone by children and dogs tagging their heels as Greensboro turned out to watch the invasion and pick up blank cartridge shells from the crowded streets.

The Army Air Force opened Basic Training Center 10 in Greensboro on March 1, 1943. The camp closed in 1946. (Courtesy Greensboro Historical Museum.)

Locations taken during the "invasion" were the buildings at Jefferson Square, the Southern Railway Station, the O. Henry Hotel, the King Cotton Hotel, City Hall, the post office, the fire department, the bus station, the courthouse, the telephone building, and the telegraph office. Mock casualties were brought by army ambulance to the first aid station on the courthouse lawn. This "invasion" was used to promote a film, *This Is the Army*, which premiered at the Carolina Theater with a Basic Training Camp 10 show, "On the Wing." Among other exercises, the residents participated in a near perfect blackout on January 13, 1944.

Among the well-known people sent to Basic Training Camp 10 was Charlton Heston. While waiting for his overseas assignment, his fiancee, Lydia Marie Clarke, came to Greensboro, and they were married in the Grace United Methodist Church on West Market Street on March 17, 1944.

At the end of the war, when Germany surrendered, Basic Training Camp 10 became a redistribution center for personnel. When Japan surrendered on August 14, 1945, it became a separation center, discharging up to 500 soldiers a day. It took a little over a year to completely vacate the barracks and close down the facility.

Greensboro honored its dead servicemen at a special ceremony on "Recognition Day," which was held at War Memorial Stadium on November 6, 1946. Later, the American Legion helped raise the funds to build a coliseum complex, and the auditorium was named Memorial Auditorium.

Greensboro citizens' enthusiastic purchase of war bonds contributed two warships to the battle against Germany and Japan. The USS *Kephart* was christened in Charleston, South Carolina, and honored Lieutenant William Perry Kephart of Greensboro, who was killed on October 14, 1942, at Guadalcanal. The USS *Greensboro* was built by the American Shipbuilding Company of Cleveland, Ohio. Both ships were launched in February 1944.

Three citizens in Guilford County gained fame during the war. Harriet Elliott, dean of students at Women's College, became the consumer adviser on the National Defense Advisory Commission from May 1940 to November 1941. In 1942, Elliott was part of the commission investigating the development of a women's auxiliary for the navy. She was instrumental in organizing the WAVES and the women's division of the War Bonds Program. In 1945, she was a delegate to the conference that ultimately set up UNESCO (the United Nations Educational, Scientific, and Cultural Organization). After her death in 1947, the student union building on the campus of Women's College was named in her memory.

Mary Webb Nicholson qualified for her private pilot's license in 1928 and became the first licensed female pilot in North Carolina. She qualified as a transport pilot in 1936. When the war began, she and 23 other female pilots were trained by the British Royal Air Force to transport Canadian planes to England. Unfortunately, on May 22, 1943, she was killed while flying over a combat area.

Major George E. Preddy from Greensboro was one of the greatest heroes of the war. As a pilot of a P-40 Warhawk, he flew in the Pacific theater. He recuperated in Australia after being wounded and was reassigned to the Eighth Air Force in England, where he was credited with destroying 23 planes. After shooting down six German planes within five minutes in August 1944, he became America's leading "ace." He was killed on December 25, 1944, while in pursuit of a German plane over Belgium by American antiaircraft fire. Preddy Boulevard is named in his honor and in honor of his brother, William, who was also killed in action.

In 1946, the army property was offered for sale. A&T College purchased 52 acres and the hospital building. A company named Bessemer Improvement Company bought most of the land and buildings for only $200,000. An entirely new neighborhood grew up, complete with businesses, shopping areas, and homes. The Summit Shopping Center was the first shopping center in Greensboro and only the second one in North Carolina.

In the post-war years, suburbs were booming. Actually, many seemingly new neighborhoods had long been developed. Between the Great Depression and the war, many projects had been cut short or cancelled. There was a pent-up demand for housing throughout the county. The post-war years brought a huge growth of single-family homes and apartments. The Federal Housing Authority helped with the construction of affordable family living spaces, and the Henry Louis Smith Homes and the Morningside Homes were built. Hunter Hills, Ardmore, and Audubon Park were developed as reasonably priced neighborhoods. This surge in construction relieved the housing shortage and created a demand for architects and contractors. Housing developments in Greensboro included Irving Park, Starmount, Hamilton Lakes, and Sedgefield.

In the 1960s and 1970s, Greensboro's downtown faded; commercial and industrial business did not return until the 1980s, revitalizing the area with high-rise office buildings. The growth of neighborhoods outside the inner city and the demand for consumer items by those new areas brought about the development of Friendly Shopping Center and Four Seasons Town Center, which was envisioned by Joe Khoury, Greensboro's most prolific builder after World War II. In the 1950s and 1960s, Khoury partnered with Bill Kirkman in developing subdivisions. He diversified into apartments and shopping centers. Khoury purchased land throughout Greensboro in anticipation of future growth. Kirkman and Khoury became the largest single-family home builder in the history of the county. In the 1970s, Khoury bought out Kirkman, and the Four Seasons Mall became his first major development.

The years after the war brought a greater use of air transportation and sales of automobiles soared. The increased popularity of these modes of transportation caused a general decline in railroad service in the county. As the number of trains decreased, so did the support services. The newsstands and restaurants closed. Some tracks fell into disuse. Amtrak was organized in 1971 and Southern stayed on operating only one passenger train, "the Southern Crescent," until 1979. At that point, the Greensboro station was donated to the City of Greensboro and the High Point station was turned into a restaurant.

Jamestown retained its small-town flavor, and for a few years in the 1980s was thought of as not only a buffer between High Point and Greensboro, but also as a bedroom community, particularly for Greensboro. In the 1990s, the town came into its own with the development of one after another large housing developments. This upward trend in population established the need for larger schools, shopping centers, and shops that would lend a degree of self-sufficiency to the community. In 2001, a new fire station was constructed and the neighborhoods have continued to grow.

The Sedgefield community was established southwest of Greensboro in the 1920s and featured a resort hotel, seen here. (Courtesy North Carolina Office of Archives and History.)

The Guilford Industrial Education Center was established in September 1963 to help prepare residents for job openings created by the growth of the many industrial companies that were constructing facilities in the county. The main campus in Jamestown opened at the site of the old Guilford County Tuberculosis Sanatorium, which operated between 1924 and 1955. In July 1983, the State Board of Community Colleges approved adding a college transfer program, and the center's name changed to Guilford Technical Community College (GTCC). The growth of GTCC has been phenomenal, with programs offered in one-year vocational and two-year technical programs. Many new classroom buildings have replaced the old structure, and satellite campuses operate in Greensboro, High Point, and at the Piedmont Triad International Airport.

High Point's shopping area on Main Street relocated to malls and specialty shops. In the 1990s, the inner city became the showrooms for furniture buyers and the home to the twice yearly furniture market, hosting as many as 50,000 visitors and buyers.

By 1928, Vicks VapoRub was established in more than 60 foreign countries, and new products were added to its original line. Over the years, creative advertising was used to launch the products into multi-million dollar sales. In 1937, the company had 2 manufacturing plants in the United States, and by 1972, there were 14 plants in the United States and 30 in foreign countries. From 1937 to 1948, Vicks increased its diverse operation with the acquisition of two companies in other drug fields. The William Merrell Company of Cincinnati, Ohio, was purchased, and the corporation then became known as Richardson-Merrell-Vicks. The J.T. Baker Chemical Company and Jensen Salsbery Laboratories were also acquired.

The most crucial social issues facing the county in the 1960s were race relations. High Point had attempted to face these issues in 1943, when it became the first Southern city with "colored patrolmen." The good intentions stalled. It was not until the 1960s when issues came full circle. In the midst of the Vietnam War, annexation battles, urban renewal, and liquor laws, the issue of race made national headlines on February 1, 1960, when four

On February 1, 1960, four African-American college students staged a sit-in at the "whites only" lunch counter in the Greensboro Woolworth's store. Their protest furthered the progress of the Civil Rights throughout the United States. In February 2002, a statue was erected on the North Carolina A&T State University campus in a tribute to the four: David Richmond, Franklin McCain, Ezell Blair Jr., and Joseph McNeil. (Photo by Burke Salsi.)

college students sat down at the lunch counter at Woolworth's in Greensboro and asked for service. All of the communities in the United States watched as similar protests were carried out in other towns—Durham, Raleigh, and Winston-Salem. On February 11, 1960, students from William Penn High School in High Point took seats at the South Main Woolworth's lunch counter and began the first non-college student protest.

Strong community reactions led to negotiation and truce. High Point appointed an "Inter-racial Committee" to bring peace to High Point. By 1963, white leaders boasted of progress with integrated public parks facilities and schools. In 1963, High Point was named an "All-America City" in part because of its "progress in race relations." Additional protests occurred in 1963 when marchers paraded through the Washington Street neighborhood for five nights. Young white bystanders jeered, and on the fifth night, smoke bombs and rocks were thrown. In response, a "Biracial Committee" was formed and charged with the expedition of the integration process. This was led by Capus Waynick, who had returned to High Point to retire. He had served as the United States ambassador to Nicaragua and Columbia. There was still little progress from the committee, and with more protests, more meetings were held with three items on the agenda: 1. Mass demonstrations would be called off; 2. the city council would not proceed with protest laws; 3. the city would create a permanent "Human Relations Commission."

Representatives for the local chapters of CORE and NAACP announced their satisfaction of the progress and from that point on, Guilford County has made gradual and steady progress for the good of all citizens regardless of color.

11. The Future Is Now

Guilford continues to be a thriving county of ever-developing industrial and commercial opportunities. The towns and cities that flourished in the 1800s continue to be the centers of the largest growth. Seamless ribbons of urban and industrial development now connect all of the once small rural towns and hamlets. The county's progress has continued as industrial, sales, and technological companies are developed or move to the county. The educational institutions established in the nineteenth century have prospered and now attract students from all over the world. Guilford Technical Community College, High Point University, the University of North Carolina at Greensboro, and North Carolina A&T State University have further supported the county by developing specialized programs to support local industry.

Textiles, tobacco, and furniture industries have made it through wars, local upheavals, droughts, recession, depression, labor shortages, and lack of transportation. Yet, in 2001, nothing prepared the citizens for the loss of jobs in each of these sectors, or the announcement that there is a continuing drop in the number of young people living in the county. Business and political leaders had immediate concerns that downturns in the once strong traditional businesses could have a negative impact on new companies considering Guilford for new sites.

Despite the undermining of the lower-end divisions of furniture by the availability of cheap labor in other countries, the furniture industry fared better at the turn of the twenty-first century than tobacco and textiles. High Point has managed to hold on to its position in manufacturing and marketing. The vision for a furniture exposition in High Point was planted at the turn of the twentieth century. The beginnings of a furniture market to attract buyers from all over the world were developed decade to decade until almost High Point's entire downtown area was devoted to showrooms. In the 1970s, the Tomlinson Chair Factory buildings were renovated into showroom space for home furnishings, and the property developed into Market Square. In 1984, there was 100,000 square feet of space. The Holiday Inn, the Furniture Plaza, and the Hamilton Market building were acquired. In 1990, the owners of Market Square opened Market Square Towers, a 15-story building of showrooms, office space, and residential condominiums.

The High Point National Furniture Mart is now a nine-story landmark, and the International Home Furnishing Market now defines the city of High Point. The small regional show that was begun a hundred years ago has become a wholesale market event that attracts over 80,000 people for eight to ten days each April and October. The High Point downtown area now features over 10 miles of space for promoting and showing furniture.

Tobacco farmers and manufacturers have experienced a slow demise in the once vibrant industry that was the future of the county in 1860. Tobacco companies continue to provide thousands of jobs throughout the Piedmont; however, the industry is plagued with problems, including health issues, legal wrangling, government restrictions on farmers, and gradual downsizing.

On the flip side, Lorillard Tobacco Company opened "the most modern cigarette plant in the world" in April 1956. The project brought $2 million in construction payrolls to Guilford County and was the largest privately financed project ever undertaken in North Carolina. Over the years, additions have been added and the facility now has a total of 1,094,544 square feet and covers 25.1 acres. The facility recently began a multi-year, multi-million-dollar equipment upgrade. The plant operates two shifts and is capable of producing 8,000 cigarettes per minute, with instruments to measure the weight of the cigarettes and inspect for defects while in operation.

Lorillard has completed the largest expansion program ever undertaken in Guilford County. In 1996, construction of a $11 million distribution center was completed. A $17 million, 124,000-square-foot facility opened in September 1997. In the same year, the company constructed a new building, relocated its corporate headquarters from New York to Greensboro, and transferred 250 employees.

Textile and apparel industries in the county have fought for over a decade to stay viable, yet have slowly faded. In 2001, Guilford County reeled from the announcements that Burlington Industries, the textile giant, and the VF Corporation, maker of brand-name apparel, including Wrangler Jeans, were in trouble. A takeover debacle at

Lorillard Tobacco Company has had manufacturing facilities in Greensboro since 1956. The new headquarters building was constructed in 1997. (Courtesy Lorillard Tobacco Company.)

146

Burlington Industries in the 1980s started peeling away at the corporate structure until the announcement in November 2001, when the textile giant was declaring bankruptcy. The apparel industry has spent decades promoting "Made in the USA," only to continue to lose jobs to emerging foreign economies that have invested in textiles and have cheap labor available. In the light of the industry's struggles, VF announced the lay-off of 13,000 workers nationwide.

Cone Mills began diversifying in 1961 by manufacturing polyurethane foam and decorative fabrics. In the 1970s, Cone formed the Cornwallis Development Company and developed unimproved real estate that had been held from Ceasar Cone's early-1900s acquisitions. During the 1980s real estate boom, the property became Ascot Point, Lake Herman, Lake Jeanette, Proximity, and Revolution. In 1997, the company was sold and Cone Mills returned its focus to textiles. In 1996, Cone Mills made a giant step toward the millennium by moving into a new $7 million corporate headquarters building. The company continues to operate three principal business segments. It is the largest producer of denim fabrics in the world and the largest commissioned printer of home-furnishing fabrics in the United States.

When J. Spencer Love returned home to Burlington, North Carolina, after serving in World War I, he raised the money to purchase a mill. He first produced flag cloth, bunting, cotton scrims, dress fabrics, and "birdseye" diaper cloth. As the demand for cotton waned, Love experimented with rayon and produced a silk-like fabric. The company made its mark becoming the national leader in rayon textiles. In 1953, Burlington Industries moved to Greensboro to take advantage of the rail system.

Through the years Burlington Industries became a giant in textiles by manufacturing everything from yarn to apparel fabrics to carpets and mattress ticking. They ran plants in seven states and Mexico and operated a merchandising office in New York. In 1987, the corporation was left in debt after an attempted takeover. The company was forced to downsize by selling off divisions. The company recovered and sales climbed to over $2.2 billion, continuing to make it one of the largest and most diversified manufacturers of textile products in the world.

Precision Fabrics Group specializes in the development of technologically advanced products and was one of the divisions sold by Burlington. It has become one of the largest textile finishing plants in the United States. They are known for the production of fabrics relating to the medical and aerospace industries, including parachute fabric, specialized filtration fabric, and protective apparel for medical purposes. They revolutionized the supplemental safety restraint industry by creating the Precision Fabrics' Precision Technology Airbag, which was named one of the top 100 inventions by Popular Science magazine in 1995.

Precision Fabrics became part of the Carter Center's Global 2000 project to eradicate the Guinea worm disease. Many people in underdeveloped areas in Asia, Southern Europe, the Middle East, and Africa dip their drinking water from non-flowing surface water. Water fleas and Guinea worm larvae are ingested with the water. The Guinea worm disease is centuries old and continues to cause incapacitation, crippling, and death. By 1990, 3.5 million people were afflicted each year. Precision Fabrics Group developed a special technical filtration fabric to fit over water jars to completely filter out water fleas and thus the larvae of the Guinea worm. The company partnered with DuPont and the Carter Center and created a 30-denier nylon monofilament yarn and then undertook the process of creating a woven fabric. Monofilament yarns are technically challenging to weave, and at the time, they had never been woven in the United States.

Other old traditional businesses of Guilford County have continued to flourish, yet in restructured forms. In 1985, Richardson-Merrell (the makers of Vicks products) was sold to Proctor and Gamble, a leading consumer goods company in Cincinnati, Ohio. Proctor and Gamble was founded in 1837, when William Proctor, a candle maker from England, and James Gamble, a soap maker from Cincinnati, formed a partnership and sold products house to house using a wheelbarrow. After the sale, Proctor and Gamble continued manufacturing Vicks products at two plants in the county—Greensboro and Brown Summit. They make deodorants, antiperspirants, toothpaste, Vicks 44, Dayquil, Fixodent, and respiratory products.

Jefferson-Pilot Life Insurance Company in Greensboro was formed on January 1, 1987, when Jefferson Standard Life and Pilot Life merged. At the time, the assets of Jefferson-Pilot Life were $3.2 billion. The new company was strengthened by its ability to provide greater insurance and financial services. With $38 billion of life insurance in force, Jefferson-Pilot Life immediately ranked in the top 2 percent of all the nation's stockholder-owned life insurance companies. Two more acquisitions in 1995 and 1997 brought the company's combined agent field force to more than 25,000.

The two corporate buildings stand side by side in the center of Greensboro. The Jefferson Building was added to the National Register of Historic Places in 1976, becoming the first commercial structure in North Carolina to be so named. A new

The Jefferson Standard Life Building, seen here c. 1955, was placed on the National Register of Historic Places in 1976.

20-story Jefferson-Pilot building was dedicated in August 1990 and is the tallest structure in Greensboro. It was designed to complement the historic Jefferson Building, as was the 860-space parking deck.

In the mid-1990s, business and political leaders came to loggerheads over solutions for correcting and directing the economy. Local business leaders and six foundations supporting non-profit corporations were concerned about having a plan for the future before there was a crisis; they commissioned a McKinsey report to study the state of and future outlook of Greensboro.

When released in late 2000, the report confirmed many disturbing aspects of the business climate. Directors of the six foundations organized task forces under a single entity aptly named Action Greensboro. The task forces were organized by topic and met to discuss issues, to define goals, and to develop recommendations. These groups were encouraged by civic leaders and local government leaders and were boosted by more than 1,200 Action Greensboro volunteers. They all shared a goal of raising the quality of life for all and attracting more and better-paying jobs.

The headline "City to get shot in the arm" was bold and black under the masthead of the *Greensboro News and Record* on Friday, February 1, 2002. Media in three counties trumpeted the announcement that Action Greensboro will spend $37 million in a three-year plan to boost the city of Greensboro's economy, improve the city's image, recruit for better jobs, and revitalize the downtown district. Beginning in the summer of 2002, plans will proceed for a new downtown park to be called Freedom Park, with a rotunda building for public and private meetings and events, and a new downtown minor-league ballpark. Millions will be spent on job recruitment, small-business growth, an image campaign, and $4 million to assist the completion of the International Civil Rights Museum.

High Point has not countered with plans so grand; however, they share a common desire to increase business activity in downtown to benefit year-round residents and complement the area occupied by furniture wholesalers and retailers. Both cities share a focus of beautification, quality of life, and attracting business to the county.

Transportation continues to be at the center of Guilford County's future. Two major interstate highways, I-40 and I-85, connect the county to all areas of the United States. Interstate 785 is under development and will open a greater north/south connection. High Point is completing the US 311 Bypass, a $35 million project that will extend from the northern city limits to US 220 in Randolph County. According to Martha Clontz, a writer for the *High Point Enterprise* (July 30, 2000), this accomplishment represents the largest road-building project the City has ever undertaken. The irony of the new bypass is that it was conceived to alleviate the traffic on Main Street, which was laid over the roadbed of the old plank road.

Trains are an important part of the daily scene and connect the county north, south, east, and west. The Norfolk Southern Corporation's north-south mainline is the busiest in the entire state and serves many industries on its routes. There are between 20 and 40 trains per day traveling through Guilford County. The company uses part of the old North Carolina Railroad between Greensboro and Raleigh as part of a lease agreement. There continues to be a large Norfolk Southern yard located in Greensboro. The railroad may again fulfill transportation needs the way it did in the nineteenth century. There is a need for a high-speed rail service route to connect Washington and Charlotte by way of Greensboro and Raleigh.

When the *Greensboro Daily News* and the *Greensboro Record* merged on March 19, 1984, the media made a step toward the future. The eighties brought a nationwide trend toward the development of 24-hour news services, and most morning and evening newspapers within the same market throughout the country merged. Eleven years later, the *Greensboro News and Record* became part of the Internet with a new service called Infinet, a regional Internet-access provider. The *News* is now a 24-hour news provider, operating a web page on the Infinet called The Depot.

Positive changes in the county in the past decades include minority residents, as well as females, gaining equal educational and employment opportunities. The progress has opened the door for minorities to gain a greater political voice and become recognized for their contributions to the county and state. Judy Mendenhall became High Point's first female mayor in 1985. She helped to initiate economic development and investment into major projects. She encouraged the development of the Piedmont Center Business Park, which continues to thrive and expand.

The citizens of Greensboro elected Carolyn Allen to be the first woman mayor in 1993. She served on the city council as mayor *pro tem* and then completed two terms as mayor. Allen was a champion of land use planning and was a member of the Land Use Task Force for Greensboro Visions. She continues her involvement with regional organizations, including the Piedmont Land Conservancy.

Dr. Patricia A. Sullivan became chancellor of the University of North Carolina at Greensboro in January 1995. She works to make UNCG a "student-centered" university and puts emphasis on outreach. Under her direction, the University launched the Center for the Study of Social Issues to utilize the faculty's expertise in solving community problems. The Center for Global Business Education and Research was established in the Joseph M. Bryan School of Business and Economics in 1996. In 1999, a $23.4 million School of Music building was completed.

Many African Americans have risen to prominent positions as county commissioners, police chiefs, and city council members. Sammie Chess of High Point was the first African-American Superior Court judge appointed in the South in the twentieth century. Henry Frye of Greensboro became the first African American elected to the North Carolina Legislature in the twentieth century, the first African-American justice of the North Carolina Supreme Court, and the first African-American Chief Justice of the Supreme Court. His wife, Shirley, became the first African-American president of the Greensboro YWCA.

Since the 1980s, much emphasis has been placed on historical preservation through the work of various associations, museums, neighborhoods, churches, and individuals. Both High Point Historical Museum and the Greensboro Historical Museum are repositories of images, artifacts, and textual documents that are the basis for the area's history. The Jamestown Historical Society is the guardian of historical sites, including the Mendenhall Plantation and Dr. Lindsay's Medical Office.

When the University of North Carolina at Greensboro announced plans to demolish the 79-year-old former chancellor's house designed by Harry Barton, it was met with

Sammie Chess of High Point was the first African-American Superior Court judge appointed in the South in the twentieth century. (Courtesy High Point Historical Museum.)

protests by university supporters. It served as the chancellor's home from the 1920s. Preservation North Carolina stepped in to raise over $1 million with plans to move the structure to another location and renovate it for an admissions and visitors center.

Preservation North Carolina is also assisting with restoration plans for Dudley High School in Greensboro. The Guilford County School System met with resistance when they announced plans to raze the school building and replace it with a new $21 million high school. Dudley's dedicated alumni wish to save the building that was North Carolina's first public high school for black students. The supporters believe the structure can be renovated, thereby preserving history and providing a modern facility for students.

After several years of personal and political upheavals and stalled donations, North Carolina Agricultural & Technical State University (NCA&T) announced a partnership with the Sit-In Museum, now named the International Civil Rights Museum. The museum will be a vital link to the county's past and will be a focal point of the continued revitalization of downtown Greensboro.

The long-planned museum was established on Elm Street in Greensboro in the original site of the old Woolworth Building. The NCA&T announcement brought new confidence to the project, and in June 2001, a resurgence of cleaning, painting, and fund-raising began. On February 1, 2002, Action Greensboro announced $4 million in support toward the completion of the museum and the hiring of a curator and director. The museum is expected to open in 2005.

The High Point Museum began renovation and expansion in 1994 that culminated in the opening of a modern interpretive museum on May 5, 2001. The $2 million project resulted from a partnership of the City of High Point, the High Point Historical Society, and private donations. The facility houses over 15,000 artifacts and documents that represent all aspects of High Point's life from pre-colonial times to the present.

The museum features a gallery entitled, "Scrapbook of History," which depicts the development of the community. The Hall of Commerce showcases local business histories and outlines their contributions to the economic development of the area.

Many preservation projects abound, renewing the culture and history of the county. The name O. Henry lives on in many forms of expression. The greatest example of forwarding his legacy and celebrating Greensboro as his birthplace was the construction of the O. Henry Hotel. Quaintance-Weaver built the new hotel as a tribute to the man, the history of the area, and followed the tradition of the grand old O. Henry Hotel, which was opened on Bellemeade in 1919. Dennis and Nancy King Quaintance and their partner, Mike Weaver, recognized the need for a locally owned hotel that would be "in and of" the community. They envisioned the new hotel as a place for local people to meet and dine as well as an elegant comfortable retreat for travelers. The stunning facade captures the grandeur of the old hotel and is detailed with features adapted from other local buildings, including the Aycock School. The spirit of the grand epoch is captured in the minute attention to detail in guestrooms. An afternoon tea is served between 2:00 and 5:00 p.m., and regular literary roundtables are presented throughout the year.

Established in honor of Greensboro's favorite son, the O. Henry Festival is hosted by Greensboro College every two years. Outstanding authors and books are presented over a four-day event opened to the public. Children learn more about books, authors, reading, and writing at the annual Piedmont Children's Book Festival, held in the Bluford Library at NCA&T every March.

The arts have become a focus of the cultural picture of Guilford County. Ballet, orchestra, theater, art galleries, and museums abound. Most of the colleges and universities boost

The O. Henry Hotel opened on Green Valley Road in 1999. The architect captured elements of the original 1919 O. Henry Hotel structure. (Courtesy Quaintance-Weaver; photo by Greg Loflin.)

The Greensboro Historical Museum is housed in the old First Presbyterian Church. (Photo by Jim Dollar.)

culture through fine arts programs, faculty presentations, and live theater. High Point is home of the professional Shakespeare Theatre Company, and Greensboro celebrated the opening of a professional theater, Triad Theatre Company, in January 2002.

The Greensboro Historical Museum was organized in 1924 and first occupied the basement of the Carnegie Public Library. The Richardson Center was created after the Richardson family purchased the First Presbyterian Church building. At first, the facility was developed to house the museum, along with the public library and other arts organizations. As other groups vacated the facility, room became available for a variety of historical collections. In 1964, a new public library was constructed, and the center became the Greensboro Historical Museum. The museum is supported by the City of Greensboro and by a non-profit group, the Greensboro Historical Museum, Inc., which owns the collections and sponsors programs.

Blandwood, the home of Governor John Motley Morehead, has been restored to its mid-1800s appearance. It is the oldest example of Italianate architecture in the United States and is a National Historic Landmark. Morehead's great-great-granddaughter, Mary Lewis Rucker Edmunds, served as chairman of the restoration committee. She said, "We literally snatched Blandwood from demolition." The project began in 1963, and the residence was dedicated in 1976.

Tannenbaum Historic Park tells the story of everyday life in the backcountry during the late 1700s. The park, the Colonial Heritage Center, and the Hoskins House are funded by Greensboro Parks and Recreation. There are hands-on exhibits, living history presentations, and special exhibits.

Guilford Courthouse National Military Park has made numerous improvements since the original Battleground Company conceived the plan to preserve the battlefield. The park attracts walkers and bicyclists and can also be viewed by taking a self-guided auto tour over the 2.25-mile road around the park. Twenty-eight monuments are dotted throughout the landscape and commemorate individuals and causes. The visitor's center houses a new exhibit opened in 2001.

Overall, the county continues to be a transportation hub of trains, planes, and trucks, and leads the technological age with the location of industries that are involved in wireless communications, circuits, and computers.

In the past, the infrastructure of the county has been dynamic enough to rebound and re-focus its vision. With transportation a key element in business, the county has continued to improve by attracting diverse businesses, including RF Micro Devices, Syngenta Crop Protection, Lucent Technologies, and Unifi. Federal Express will start construction on a $300 million package-sorting hub at the Piedmont Triad Airport by 2005.

It is astounding to see how many neighborhoods have grown up in the past 20 years. The county population is composed of many nationalities and people from every state in the United States, who have brought their skills and expertise to enhance the economic picture of the county. The drive west to Winston-Salem and east to Burlington is one connective strip of neighborhoods, industry, office parks, retail shopping, and fast-food restaurants joining Guilford to Forsyth and Alamance Counties almost as one. What was once a two-day carriage drive has been reduced to 30 minutes, thanks to the visions and determination of men and women who reached beyond their personal comfort for the good of their homes, neighborhoods, and cities to make Guilford County the very heart of the Piedmont.

This 2001 view of Greensboro shows the city's progress and diversity. (Photo by Jim Dollar.)

ENDNOTES

CHAPTER ONE

1. Hilty, Hiram. *New Garden Friends Meeting: The Christian People Called Quakers.* p. 3
2. Connor, R.D.W. *North Carolina Rebuilding an Ancient Commonwealth: 1584–1925.* p. 18.
3. Week, S.B. *Southern Quakers.* p. 34.
4. DeCrevecoeur, J. Hector St. John. *Letters from an American Farmer.* p. 78.
5. Connor, R.D.W. *North Carolina Rebuilding an Ancient Commonwealth: 1584–1925.* pp. 16–17.

CHAPTER TWO

1. Baker, Thomas E. *Another Such Victory.* p. 11.
2. Newlin, Algie. *The Battle of New Garden.* pp. 31–33.

CHAPTER THREE

1. Arnett, Ethel Stephens. *Greensboro, North Carolina: The County Seat of Guilford.*
2. Connor, R.D.W. *North Carolina Rebuilding an Ancient Commonwealth: 1584–1925.* Vol. II. p. 31.
3. Stockard, Sallie W. *The History of Guilford County, North Carolina.* p. 60.

CHAPTER FOUR

1. "Plank Road Exhibit." High Point Museum.

CHAPTER FIVE

1. Arnett, Ethel Stephens. *Greensboro, North Carolina: The County Seat of Guilford.* p. 391.
2. ibid., p. 392.
3. "Stoneman's Raid: March 23–April 26, 1865." *United States Civil War.* www.us-civilwar.com
4. Robinson, Blackwell P. *History of Guilford County.* Vol. I. p. 110.

CHAPTER SIX

1. Arnett, Ethel Stephens. *Greensboro, North Carolina: The County Seat of Guilford.* p. 149.
2. Stockard, Sallie W. *The History of Guilford County, North Carolina.* p. 136.

CHAPTER SEVEN

1. Arnett, Ethel Stephen. *O. Henry from Polecat Creek.* p. 129.
2. Stockard, Sallie W. *The History of Guilford County, North Carolina.* pp. 92–94.

3. *Normal and Industrial School Annual Catalogue*. Vol. I. p. 16.

CHAPTER EIGHT

1. Stoesen, Alexander R. *History of Guilford County*. Vol. II. p. 176.
2. ibid., p. 171.

CHAPTER NINE

1. Stoesen, Alexander R. *History of Guilford County*. Vol. II. p. 181.
2. Cone Mills Centennial Committee. *Cone: A Century of Excellence, the History of Cone Mills 1891 to 1991.*

Seen at its dedication on July 6, 1933, the federal building and post office was constructed on the corner of Market and Eugene in 1931. (Courtesy Farrell Collection, North Carolina Office of Archives and History.)

BIBLIOGRAPHY

Books

Arnett, Ethel Stephens. *Greensboro, North Carolina: The County Seat of Guilford*. Chapel Hill: the University of North Carolina Press, 1955.

———. *O. Henry from Polecat Creek*. Greensboro: Greensboro Printing Co., 1966.

———. *The Saura and Keyauwee in the Land that Became Guilford, Randolph, and Rockingham*. Greensboro: Media, Inc., 1975.

———. *William Swain: Fighting Editor*. Greensboro: Piedmont Press, 1963.

Baker, Thomas E. *Another Such Victory*. Eastern National, 1999.

———. *The Monuments at Guilford Courthouse National Military Park*. National Park Service.

Banner, Ray R. *Greensboro: The Best Place to Live*. Self-published, 1998.

Bowles, Elisabeth Ann. *A Good Beginning: The First Four Decades of the University of North Carolina at Greensboro*. Chapel Hill: the University of North Carolina Press, 1967.

Coffin, Levi. *Reminiscences of Levi Coffin*. Cincinnati, OH: Robert Clark and Co., 1880.

Connor, R.D.W. *North Carolina Rebuilding an Ancient Commonwealth: 1584–1925*. Volumes I–IV. Chicago: American Historical Society, 1929.

Crow, Jeffrey J., Paul D. Escatt, and Flora J. Hatley. *A History of African Americans in North Carolina*. Raleigh: North Carolina Division of Archives and History, 1992.

Edmunds, Mary Lewis Rucker. *Recollections of Greensboro*. 1993.

Hilty, Hiram H. *New Garden Friends Meeting: The Christian People Called Quakers*. New Garden: North Carolina Friends Historical Society, 1983.

Hinshaw, Seth B., and Mary Ethel Hinshaw. *Carolina Quakers: Our Heritage Our Hope Tercentenary 1672-1972*.

Johnson, Clint. *Touring the Carolinas' Civil War Sites*. Winston-Salem: John F. Blair Publishers, 1996.

Jones, Abe D. Jr. *Greensboro 27*. Bassett, VA: Bassett Printing Co., 1976.

Lawson, John. *A New Voyage to Carolina*. Hugh Talmage Lefler, ed. Chapel Hill: the University of North Carolina Press.

Marks, Robert. *High Point Reflections of the Past*. Montgomery, AL: Community Communications, Inc., 1996.

Newlin, Algie. *The Battle of New Garden*. Greensboro: 1977.

O'Keefe, Patrick. *Greensboro: A Pictorial History*. Virginia Beach, VA: Donning Company Pub., 1977.

Powell, William S. *North Carolina: A History*. Chapel Hill: the University of North Carolina Press, 1988.

Robinson, Blackwell P. *History of Guilford County*. Vol. I. Greensboro: Guilford County Bicentennial Commission, 1971.

St. John deCrevecoeur, J. Hector. *Letters from an American Farmer*. New York: Dutton Pub., 1912.

Salsi, Lynn, and Frances Eubanks. *Images of America: Carteret County*. Charleston, SC: Arcadia Publishing, 1999.

Scarlette, Gladys. *Summerfield, North Carolina: A Pictorial History*. Battleground Printing and Publishing, 1999.

Sills, Walter H. *Old Times Not Forgotten*. Greensboro: Cedar Bend Printing, 1991.

Silcox-Jarrett, Diane. *Charlotte Hawkins Brown*. Winston-Salem: Bandit Books, 1995.

Stockard, Sallie W. *The History of Guilford County, North Carolina*. Knoxville, TN: Gaut-Ogden Company Printers and Book Binders, 1902.

Stoesen, Alexander R. *Guilford College: On the Strength of 150 Years*. Greensboro: Trustees of Guilford College, 1987.

———. *Guilford County: A Brief History*. Durham: N.C. Division of Archives and History, 1993.

———. *History of Guilford County*. Vol. II. Greensboro: Guilford Co. Bicentennial Comm., 1971.

Thane, Elswyth. *The Fighting Quaker: Nathanael Greene*. Mallicluck, NY: Amereon House, 1977.

Week, S.B. *Southern Quakers*. Reprinted: New York: Bergman Publishers, 1968.

Newspapers

The *Greensboro Daily News*

The *Greensboro Daily Record*

The *Greensboro News and Record*

The *Greensboro Patriot*

The *High Point Enterprise*

The *Times* (Greensboro)

Primary Sources and Miscellaneous

Cone Mills Centennial Committee. *Cone: A Century of Excellence, the History of Cone Mills 1891 to 1991*. Greensboro: Cone Mills Centennial Committee, 1991.

Dr. McIver's Letters / Mrs. McIver's Letters. Rare Book Room, Jackson Library, University of North Carolina at Greensboro.

Harris, Donald. Interview. May 2, 2001.

Harris, Jean. Interview. May 3, 2001.

Holder, Janice. Interview. June 2001.

Normal and Industrial School Annual Catalogue. Vol. I. 1892–1893.

Parnell, Charles. Interview. June 2001.

Proceedings Board of Directors, Normal and Industrial School, Office of the Superintendent of Public Instruction. Raleigh: 1891–1892.

Sharpe, Charlie. Interview. May 10, 2001.

"Stoneman's Raid: March 23–April 26, 1865." *United States Civil War*. http://www.us-civilwar.com.

INDEX

ABOUT THE AUTHOR

Lynn Salsi is a full-time historian, documentary writer, and children's author. She was a 2001 winner of the American Library Association Notable Book Award and was named 2001 North Carolina Historian of the Year (West) by the North Carolina Society of Historians. She is the recipient of the Willie Parker Peace History Book Award and the Paul Green Multi Media Award.

Lynn is the author of three Arcadia books: *Images of America: Carteret County*; *Images of America: Craven County*; and *Voices of America: The Crystal Coast*.

ABOUT THE RESEARCHER

Burke Salsi has worked as photo editor and researcher on several of Lynn's projects, including the *North Carolina Imagination Box*, *From Murphy to Manteo*, and *Glenn Bolick's Appalachian ABC's*. In this book, he teamed with Jim Dollar to produce excellent photographs of current preservation projects, renovations, and new construction.

This c. 1937 aerial view illustrates the dynamic growth of the city of Greensboro and thus, Guilford County. The Foust Administration Building and College Avenue are visible in the foreground on the right. (Courtesy University Archives and Manuscripts, Jackson Library, University of North Carolina at Greensboro.)